A Packet of Cigarettes

Mike Wheeler

First published by Ultimate World Publishing 2025
Copyright © 2025 Michael Wheeler

ISBN

Hardback: 978-1-923425-31-6
Ebook: 978-1-923425-32-3

Michael Wheeler has asserted his rights under the Copyright, Designs and Patents Act 1988 to be identified as the author of this work. The information in this book is based on the author's experiences and opinions. The publisher specifically disclaims responsibility for any adverse consequences which may result from use of the information contained herein. Permission to use information has been sought by the author. Any breaches will be rectified in further editions of the book.

All rights reserved. No part of this publication may be reproduced, stored in or introduced into a retrieval system, or transmitted in any form, or by any means (electronic, mechanical, photocopying, recording or otherwise) without the prior written permission of the author. Any person who does any unauthorised act in relation to this publication may be liable to criminal prosecution and civil claims for damages. Enquiries should be made through the publisher.

Cover design: Ultimate World Publishing
Layout and typesetting: Ultimate World Publishing
Editor: Alex Floyd-Douglass
Cover Image Copyright:
Eugene_Photo-Shutterstock.com
Huy Thoai-Shutterstock.com

Ultimate World Publishing
Diamond Creek,
Victoria Australia 3089
www.writeabook.com.au

Dedication

To Thiêu and Tô Cao – for risking it all.

Foreword

I COULD NEVER IMAGINE having to leave my homeland under duress. I immigrated from NZ to Australia almost two decades ago, but the cultural leap was hardly burdensome.

Imagine you live in a country where you see no future for your children other than a subsistence existence and no chance of getting ahead in life unless you belong to the political elite.

These are the thought processes that went through Thiêu and Tô Cao's minds after the fall of Saigon to the NVA in 1975 – not that they thought they would have been any better under the corrupt South Viêtnamese regime.

The end of the Viêtnam Civil War was the catalyst that made them, and Tô's extended family, make the decision to leave Viêtnam and seek a better life elsewhere.

This book is a record of their upbringing and journey to a foreign land – the hard decisions that needed making ,and the sacrifices they underwent so the next generation and the ones after could have a better life.

Sometimes, following generations need to be reminded that they are in the lucky country due to the sacrifices made by their forebears in a Third World country, five decades ago and 5,000 kilometres away.

Acknowledgements

LIKE ANY WORTHWHILE ENDEAVOUR, it takes more than one person to make an idea a reality.

First and foremost, thank you to Thiêu and Tô Cao for allowing me to spend many Sunday afternoons recounting their journey from Viêtnam to Australia; for letting me into their lives as they talked about their upbringing, and the hard choices and worries of how life would turn out for them in this new and strange land.

To the wider Cao clan, a special thanks to my partner Dianne and her siblings for sharing sometimes painful memories of those moments when they left their homeland and settled not only in a foreign country, but one that had different cultural norms and mores. Navigating the balance between Asian values and Western cultural expectations was never easy.

Also, to Hamish McIntosh for his insight and guidance when it came to making sure the look of the book got what it deserved.

Finally, to Christine Clancy who took the script and ironed out the bumps and bruises to make it a better story.

Thank you all.

Contents

Dedication	iii
Foreword	v
Acknowledgements	vii
Chapter 1: Growing Up	1
Chapter 2: Teenage Years	11
Chapter 3: Thi Tô	21
Chapter 4: The Army	27
Chapter 5: The Fall of Saigon	36
Chapter 6: Life Under Communism	39
Chapter 7: The Boat	44
Chapter 8: Lost at Sea	48
Chapter 9: Leaving – 1977	53
Chapter 10: At Sea	59
Chapter 11: Arrival	62
Chapter 12: Camp Life	67
Chapter 13: A New Home	83
Chapter 14: The Locals	86
Chapter 15: Working	88

Chapter 16: Sydney	91
Chapter 17: Penrith	95
Chapter 18: Back in the Fold	101
Chapter 19: Family	104
Chapter 20: Cultural Values	106
Chapter 21: The Kids	110
Chapter 22: The Children's Stories	119
Epilogue	143
Appendix	145
The Children's Eulogies to Thieu	145
About the Author	155

Chapter 1

Growing Up

By the time Thiêu Cao was 14, he'd been a fisherman, wholesale food trader, house boy, and straw stacker. He had also been an orphan for more than a decade.

Like a lot of Viêtnamese – especially those in the south of the country – Thiêu was of Chinese stock. His father, Bo Kam, had fled the southern province of Guangdong after he thought he had killed a man.

The story goes that the man his father killed came from a family who had a leadership role in the village. The man and his cronies constantly teased Bo Kam because his brother was the village beggar. Every day, as he was going to work, the man and his friends would remind Bo Kam that his brother was a disgrace.

One day, Bo Kam lost his temper and hit the man. He assumed he killed him but didn't hang around to find out. Instead, he headed south via ship and landed in Southern Viêtnam. Once he disembarked, he travelled for a few days

A Packet of Cigarettes

before arriving in a small village in the far south-west – Hung Hoang – where he made his home.

This was the 1920s. Viêtnam was part of French Indochina and was divided into three separate peoples – the North Viêtnamese, the South Viêtnamese and those in the middle of the country, who were indigenous. The indigenous had been prolific throughout that part of Southeast Asia, but over time, they slowly had their land area reduced as other cultures started to intrude – mainly the Chinese from the north and the Khmer from the west. Eventually, the darker-skinned, indigenous would total about 100,000.

Thiêu was born in 1942. Growing up in rural Viêtnam in the late 1940s and early 1950s was hard. This part of Southeast Asia was in a state of flux. Looking back, Thiêu was not impressed with the French colonisers. Among some today, there is a romanticised history that the French brought civilisation to the area, along with many Western ideals and practical infrastructure. However, as far as Thiêu is concerned, the colonisers were nothing but rorters.

"The French owned the land, but they lived in the city," Thiêu says. "They would get a local to take care of the land, and that person would sublease it to tenants. However, you could never get ahead in life. You only made enough to keep your family fed, sheltered and clothed. They just sucked the money out of rural Viêtnam in the form of taxes and rents."

By 1954, the nationalistic Viét Minh had won the battle of Điện Biên Phủ, which sent the country's French masters packing back to Europe. This brought about a new set of problems for the fledgling country. It would take the best part of two decades before any conclusion to its future would be decided.

Thiêu was four years old when his father died. The country had been under the control of the French for nearly six decades, and their influence was felt throughout the land – from its

Growing Up

architecture and the development of the Viêtnamese Latin-based alphabet to the French bakeries selling pastries along the boulevards and alleyways of Hanoi and Saigon.

When Thiêu was born, the country was under Japanese control due to the acquiescence of France's Nazi-friendly Vichy regime. French Indochina had yet to be partitioned into the four countries it would eventually become – Laos in the west, Cambodia in the south, and North and South Viêtnam on the eastern seaboard.

In his village, there was no running water, no sewage, or other amenities. Water was collected from a well, or the roof when it rained. There was little law and order, and Saigon was 300km and an eight-hour bus ride away.

He was the youngest of four siblings; he had an older brother, Ty Hien, who was 12 years his senior and two sisters aged in between, the older being Thi Ba. The younger of his two sisters, Thi Kia, died when she was young, so his memory of her is minimal. He cannot remember what she died of, only that one day she was there, and then she wasn't.

Thiêu was born at a time when the country's revolutionaries were embracing Communist ideals. These principles had been entrenched into many peasants' psyches by Ho Chi Minh, who founded the Viêtnamese Communist Party in 1930. Thiêu's father had no ambitions in politics and set about being a farmer growing vegetables such as cucumber and ginger. It was a sparse life and a hard one. Once settled, Bo married Kit Duong, a young lady of Chinese and Cambodian descent.

Both of Thiêu's parents died within a short time span. Bo Kam was on his way home from another village after spending the previous three nights playing Chinese four-colour cards and drinking. He was between villages when he collapsed and never regained consciousness. Thiêu is unsure as to the cause of death but thinks it was likely a heart attack or stroke.

A Packet of Cigarettes

His mother was another story and an even sadder case. She was a chronic alcoholic.

"My grandfather on my mother's side had two children, my mother and her brother," says Thiêu. "My grandfather allowed my uncle to go to study in China. My grandmother passed away very early so my mother stayed with my grandfather. My grandfather drank a lot and didn't have friends, so he made my mother drink with him.

"She became an alcoholic. She died a few months after my father. She couldn't live without my father because he was the key to the family. My father took care of everyone, but my mother, not at all. She used to drink shots of something similar to vodka. She was a bad alcoholic."

He illustrated the extent of her affliction with an anecdote. Kit Duong used to visit a haystack next to a barn during the dry season because she used hay to cook food. One time, when Thiêu was a baby, she left him there because she was drunk, thought he was dead, and buried him in the hay and went home. She sat down and drank more to bury her sorrows at the 'death' of her son. Bo Kam came home and asked where Thiêu was. Kit told him what had happened, so Bo Kam went to the haystack and found Thiêu very much alive.

Thiêu was hard-pressed to recall how she died. He believes it was due to alcohol. From what his older sister Thi Ba told him; his mother couldn't cope with looking after the family. This led to more drinking and inevitably, her death.

With both parents now dead, his older brother, Ty Hien, was expected to take up the mantle. Asian cultures are patriarchal, and Viêtnam is no exception. While still only 16, Ty Hien was the natural choice to look after his younger siblings. He did so for a couple of years. But it didn't last long.

"Two years after my father passed away, he just up and left us. I was about six at the time and my sister was about 16. He

Growing Up

didn't see his siblings as his responsibility, so he just moved on with his life. He was surviving in his own way, I guess," says Thiêu.

His brother chose not to live in the family house and went to stay with one of their uncles in the same village because the uncle had more money. Ty Hien had his own business buying and selling products, transporting them to Saigon and back.

One day, he decided to stay in Saigon and never returned.

"He was nomadic on his own. I can't remember what he looked like. He went very early. We didn't have letters back then, so there was no way to keep in touch," Thiêu says.

Ty Hien died quite young. He was just 26. Thiêu heard from a distant relative that he was working for a shipping company that was transporting oil, and a drum fell on him. That was the end of him.

With his brother gone, it was up to Thiêu's older sister to run the household. His parents had a house that had five rooms. The front three rooms were where Thiêu and his sister lived, while the back two rooms were to be rented out. It was a dangerous enterprise for Ba.

Being a young woman, she took the risk of being abused – in many ways – by potential renters as she was alone at the time. Luckily their father had lent people some money for various businesses. Those people repaid Thi Ba, and that money was enough to survive that first year alone without having to rent the rooms out.

However, it wasn't long before Thiêu had to start paying his own way, even though he was only seven years old. Initially, it was odd jobs around the village, such as looking after children and helping around various houses. He also went fishing.

Finally, his sister decided that he would live with a family and work as a houseboy. They found a family in the same village who took him on. It was a good arrangement because they allowed him to see his sister. It was common practice in Viêtnam for families that were struggling to allow their children this type of living arrangement. Workers would get paid on a monthly or even annual basis.

While Thiêu was sure that some of these situations were open to all kinds of abuse, the family who looked after him was nice. In later years, after settling in Australia, Thiêu would visit them when he returned to Viêtnam and bring them gifts because they had treated him well. He did this until they passed away.

He also had a job where he looked after the village ox, which was used to sow crops. Animals like oxen were an important part of the village because of the work they could accomplish. This meant the animal was valuable. It was Thiêu's job to make sure nobody would steal it.

When he was 10 years old, his father's good friend sent him off to a Chinese school for a year. This person had been a friend of his father's since they were together in China.

"He sent me there because he didn't want me to lose my heritage," says Thiêu. "There are a lot of Chinese people in Viêtnam, so it was all about retaining the heritage and culture.

"I didn't do too well because I didn't study; I wasn't immersive in Mandarin. I understood Mandarin, and I spoke Viêtnamese, and Teo Cheow, a derivative of Mandarin. Teo Cheow writing is similar to Mandarin, but the way you say it and put it together is different, which meant it didn't do me any good at the school, so I had to leave after a year."

Thiêu started work for his father's friend by helping trade groceries via a boat that visited different villages up and down the waterways of the area. Thiêu was 12 years old and was responsible for loading the produce onto the boat.

"He would buy rice and wheat and then trade it. It was hard work. I learned a bit about entrepreneurship doing this. I was learning the first step to making a living," says Thiêu.

Growing Up

Thiêu's memory was a bit hazy in terms of the order in which things happened, but he does remember the boat worked well. He's not too sure what happened as to why he stopped working onboard but he remembered having poor circulation sitting on the boat all the time – he couldn't walk properly. He found the work taxing on his body.

Due to this physical nature of the work, he needed a lot of food to keep his energy levels up. However, his boss couldn't afford to feed him enough, so Thiêu ate a lot of rice husks that hadn't been processed because he thought there might be nutrients and vitamins that could make him more resilient. Protein was also hard to come by, so eventually he went back to his sister's.

"The man who owned the boat was very nice. It's like when you have a good friend and then he passes away, and you take care of his kids. That is what he did. He helped us because of the friendship he had with my father," says Thiêu.

While Thiêu was making his way in the world, and after the French defeat at Điện Biên Phủ, a new phase in Việtnam's history was about to begin. With Điện Biên Phủ being in the north-west, and Thiêu and his family being in the far south-west, these events had little immediate impact on him in his day-to-day life. Although, he recollects the French and the Communists being in and around the community.

"I remember on the odd occasion that the French might visit during the day," he recalls.

"Then the Communists would come during the night. We lived on a village near the Cambodian border. There were villages in South Việtnam that were Communist, and then the next village was anti-Communist. A lot of South Việtnamese wanted the French to stay. They didn't know much about the Americans who were starting to exert influence, and they didn't like the Communists."

A Packet of Cigarettes

Thiêu understood at the time that the Communists wanted to unite the country behind its dogma. In order to win, they started playing the long game. This started back in 1954 once the French were gone, and the country was partitioned into North and South Viêtnam along the 17th parallel.

Although some people were keen to see Ho Chi Minh rule the country, it wasn't going to happen right away. Once the partition had taken place, there was a lot of movement of people between the two countries. Many of the Communist sympathisers in the South were told by the Communist hierarchy in the North to stay where they were – they would be needed later. Thiêu believed that this type of thinking was one of the main reasons the Communists were successful in the long run. He thought that those in charge of the South's government were not thinking in those terms. They had no designs to invade the North and unite the country. Those in the North not only spoke a different dialect but also had different values.

According to Thiêu, there might be a family of 10 in the South and five went North to live under Communist rule. The five who stayed were left behind on purpose.

"The Communists were strategising already," he says. "These people, or sleepers, pretended to be for the South, but they were aligned with the North."

There was a three-month grace period where the South Viêtnamese could go to the North and vice versa. At the time, most southerners didn't realise Communists stayed behind and so were unprepared for what happened over the next two decades. Thiêu felt that South Viêtnam was under-prepared from the beginning.

In his village, no one left to go north. But in nearby villages, a few stayed behind who turned out to be Communists. Even back then, in the daytime, the South Viêtnamese military might visit, then at nighttime, the Communists would come.

Growing Up

Thiêu was 12 when the French left and the full nightmare of the Viêtnam War was still a decade away. More than a million North Viêtnamese headed south. Most were Catholics who were worried that they would be the victims of persecution by the atheist Communists.

Twelve months later, after an impasse with the Soviet Union and Chinese-based Viêtnamese Communists at the 1954 Geneva Conference, US president Dwight Eisenhower sent the first American military 'advisors' to South Viêtnam. They were there to 'train' the Republic of Viêtnam's (RVN) army. By the late 1950s, the number of US military personnel had increased to 900.

None of this affected the young Thiêu who was focussed on survival. He still worked for the family in his village as a house boy. As time went on, the type of tasks he did for them varied and included rice farming and any other chores the family could think of at the time. This wasn't some dystopian Dickenson existence.

To him, although it was a hard life, it was just life, and he was happy to have food in his belly, a roof over his head, and a family that treated him well. Once his chores were finished, he would go fishing in the nearby river to help feed his sister and her family. Even at a young age, he was industrious and would make his own fishing nets.

"I made a 5m-by-5m net," he says. "There is a lot of water in Viêtnam. That is something I would do on the side. I would take fish from the river to my sister who would sell it for other food. I caught a lot of fish."

During the transition between adolescence and adulthood, Thiêu knew he wanted to make something of his life. He had many hurdles that only someone born in this part of the world could recognise. His prospects on most fronts were bleak – he had limited education, was unskilled, an orphan, had a brother

A Packet of Cigarettes

who didn't care for his welfare and a sister that was struggling to survive herself, let alone look after a younger brother.

Talking to Thiêu almost six decades later, he doesn't see his life in those terms. He knew to get ahead in life, he needed to be better than others by taking on more responsibilities and as a result, more chances.

Chapter 2

Teenage Years

At the age of 15, Thiêu left his home village and headed south to the village of Soc Trang where a distant relative lived. The relation, a distant aunt called Lang Thi Ly, looked out for him and became his benefactor. Most people in the village were of Cambodian decent, with only few Chinese and Viêtnamese people living in the area.

It was at this time that Thiêu went through different jobs building up a career, mainly at the behest of his guardian angel, Lang.

He started as an apprentice tailor. He worked there for a week, and although he didn't last long, he did learn a few things – how to be thrifty and what hard work was all about.

"The first week, I made a pair of shorts," he says.

"The tailor told me to go and get some offcuts from a roll of fabric. He didn't waste one scrap of fabric – any piece could be made into anything he told me. I did what he told me and produced a pair of shorts."

A Packet of Cigarettes

Although he was only there for a week, Thiêu remembers that it was hard work because it was manual. He had to push the sewing machine pedal back and forth the whole day, which was very hard on the body.

Lang came and checked up on him to see how he was going. The tailor told her not let Thiêu take on the profession because he was a very skinny boy, and he thought Thiêu had bad lungs. In that environment, when a machinist is cutting and sewing, it created dust, and the tailor didn't think it was a good profession for Thiêu.

The tailor told Lang that Thiêu was a bright boy and that he had never known an apprentice one week into the job being able to make a pair of shorts.

"He said I could learn a lot of stuff, but he didn't think this profession would suit me because of the amount of labour involved," says Thiêu.

"He showed my aunt a photo of how he used to look – a nice big healthy man – and after so many years, he was now a skinny, bent old man. He saw that I was very earnest, and a quick learner and I was coachable. He advised my aunt to take me elsewhere because he was sure that whatever profession I chose I would do okay at it."

With his days as a tailor behind him, the next career move was that of a bicycle repairer. Bicycles were the transport of choice for many people in the villages and hamlets of southeast Asia. They were not expensive, required little maintenance and could get you from A to B faster than walking. The idea of working in such an industry appealed to Thiêu because he knew that there would be long-term work available. His benefactor agreed.

Once again, the idea was to work for a few weeks and, if both parties agreed, an apprenticeship would follow. There was no pay in it – as with tailoring, the labour was free in

Teenage Years

exchange for room, food and learning a trade. However, like his previous foray, the no pay aspect wasn't the issue – it was the work itself.

Both Thiêu and his aunt thought he would be learning the ins and outs of how to fix bikes. He soon realised the owner of the business wasn't looking out for Thiêu's long-term prospects but was taking advantage of free labour to do the menial work.

When starting out as an apprentice, all Thiêu was doing was shaving off the rust from the frame, filing away the old paint and getting it prepared for a new coat. He felt he didn't learn much day in and day out. He thought they only took him on because all he was doing was preparing the bike to be repaired and be repainted for free.

After a few weeks, he wanted to do other stuff. He was told that when somebody new got hired, they would get the cruddy jobs, but they promised that they would teach him a thing or two in terms of maintenance – the things he really wanted to learn. However, they took their time, because they want to keep him there sanding and filing for as long as possible. To him, it was a boring job that nobody else wanted.

Lang didn't visit Thiêu that often, but when she did come to the village, she made a point of checking on his welfare. About a month into his bicycle apprenticeship, she decided to go the village and stop in and see Thiêu before heading off to do her shopping.

When she arrived at the repair shop, she looked around and couldn't see him but didn't think much of it. A couple of hours later, after she had bought her groceries, she came back, but again, couldn't find him. This caused her concern, so she approached the shop owner and asked about Thiêu's whereabouts.

"He pointed me out to her. She didn't recognise me because I was covered in dust and grime," says Thiêu.

A Packet of Cigarettes

"I could tell she was not happy, but she was diplomatic towards the owner. Because I was living with them, she had to ask the owner if I could come home with her to dinner because she was visiting me. He said yes. When she took me back to her house, she told me not to go back there because it was not a good place for me. She said she couldn't see me doing well there and she felt that the owner mistreated me. She was watching out for me. She said he wasn't a good boss."

That was the end of Thiêu's sojourn as a bicycle repair man. His aunt's reasons were not only because she had taken a dislike towards the boss, but there were also other, aesthetic and more practical reasons Lang wanted him to move on. And it was nothing to do with working.

"She thought I was too handsome to do the job," says Thiêu with a grin.

"She said I could learn the job and learn how to be a good businessman from it. However, if I kept on doing it, I would never get a wife because I was constantly covered in soot and grime. Men should not look like that, she said."

Having tried and missed out on a few potential career paths, Thiêu was at a loose end. He had the ambition to get a job, and he had the work ethic to make the best out of what he could do, but so far nothing had worked out.

It was then that his life took a detour for the worse. Just as he ended his time at the bicycle shop, his sister's husband fell sick – he was coughing up blood. He couldn't work, so the family was in a financially difficult situation. Thiêu went back to their village to help.

His brother-in-law did backbreaking work whereby he carried shafts of rice to and from the fields. He would buy it in bulk and then sell it upriver using a boat as transport. However, when he got sick, he couldn't do that anymore. Thiêu went home for a year and took care of the business.

Teenage Years

He did that for a while and managed to save 3,000 dong. He gave the money to his sister because she had a family, and he didn't need it because he could survive on minimal food. It was 1958 and he was 16 years old. He was 55kg and each load was about 65kg. It wasn't on flat land, and he had to do about 50 trips a day loading the boat. It had no motor, so they had to row. It was 13km there and back to where the load had to be sold.

When Lang saw him, she cried. She thought he was too small, so set about trying to find him another job when his brother-in-law's health improved.

Once he was under the umbrella of Lang's tutelage again, she hit upon the idea that he should become a hairdresser. Most hairdressers in Viêtnam were men, and they usually ran the salon. Lang and her daughter were visiting a salon one day – again in Song Trac – when it came to her that this career could be a good fit for her handsome, young charge. She noticed that hairdressers were always well presented – nice shoes, debonaire trousers and a collared shirt. A nice, clean environment compared to the grimy locale of a bicycle repair shop, tailor's fitting room, or a boat.

It wasn't long before pushy Lang accosted one of the local hairdressers to give an apprenticeship to her enthusiastic nephew. Unlike Western cultures, where an apprentice is paid minimum wage to learn a job, when it came to hairdressing, the apprentice has to pay the hairdresser to spend his or her time teaching somebody a trade.

Lang was shrewd. Having already seen how Thiêu's previous experiences had turned out, she made a deal with the salon owner.

"Lang did not want to pay money at first. She said to me, 'I'll let you stay with him for a month first and see how you go'," says Thiêu.

A Packet of Cigarettes

"She wanted to see if the hairdresser was fraudulent and was only wanting the money instead of teaching me a trade. She saw me as a naive boy from the country. If I was good, she would agree to the deal. He introduced me to the head hairdresser who was a lady.

During that first month, she would say to me, 'This is how it works. This is perming agent; these are the rollers. You need to prepare these for me when I am ready, so when we have clients that are ready to do this.' However, when the month was up and my aunt handed over the 3,000 dong, things changed. They kept me at the back to do all the household duties, the kitchen hand and all the other stuff. I didn't get to do the hairdressing side."

However, Thiêu had an ally in the lead hairdresser. Not only did she run the salon, but her husband was a hairdresser at another salon. She didn't think it was fair that Thiêu wasn't given the chance to try out the things she was teaching him. Being an honest person, she came up with a plan to help Thiêu so that he could get his career underway.

His boss owned him, so he had to stay home at night-time. One day, the female hairdresser said to Thiêu's boss, "He is young and up and coming and I haven't introduced him to my husband yet. If I don't introduce him to my husband, he might come in one day and get jealous. So, I want them to meet."

"Looking back on it now," says Thiêu, "I realise that she had spoken to her husband and told him how unfair my boss was being to me. She thought it was wrong that the boss took my aunt's 3,000 dong and wouldn't teach me – that I wouldn't have a career.

"When I met her husband, he asked me how I felt about being a hairdresser. I said I wanted to do it. He asked me to quit the job and after a month, come back and look for him and he'd find me another place that will teach me for free."

Teenage Years

And that is what happened. A month later, to ensure there was no suspicion on the lady who helped him, Thiêu quit his job. He then went to her husband who introduced him to another hairdresser who was willing to teach him for free. The only caveat was that Thiêu had to provide his own food. As he wasn't getting paid, this was going to be hard.

Being resourceful, Thiêu went to the local food charity, which was run by the wives of wealthy men. He initially hit a snag because most of the men who went to the shop looked needy – they were unkempt and had ragged clothes. Thiêu turning up in his nice slacks, dress shirt and polished shoes raised the eyebrows of those in charge of the patronage.

One lady accosted him as to why he was there, and he decided the best course of action was to be honest. He knew it was a risky strategy, but it paid off. The fact that he was from the country was seen as a mitigating circumstance. She even went as far as to tell him that whenever he arrived, he must let her know he was there so she could give him extra food.

Within three months of working, Thiêu was trusted enough by the head hairdresser to be left in charge of the store while everybody else was at lunch. His working day was monotonous, but it was this type of regime a youth with no parents needed.

Once the shop opened, the owner would go and get himself a morning coffee. Thiêu was left at the store to clean up his boss's bed, sweep, mop, wipe the windows down, get the chair ready and make sure everything was in place for the day. He told Thiêu that if customers came in, he was to tell them that Thiêu was getting them ready for the boss and he would come back and cut the hair.

Thiêu observed the hairdresser for three months. He was a quick study, but he still wasn't getting paid. The hairdresser promised to start paying him in the New Year, but once the lunar calendar had come full circle – nothing. To add to Thiêu's concerns, the hairdresser had promised to advance his training. Again, this didn't happen.

His former co-worker's husband came back on the scene and saw what was happening. He agreed it wasn't fair, so took Thiêu to the side and advised him to leave. Thiêu wasn't sure at first, but knew he needed to earn money. He also knew he had taken in a lot of what he had been taught and thought he could apply it to a new job. His friend soon found him a new job with another hairdresser. A job that paid real money. Thiêu was 19 years old.

A Cultural Interlude

Chinese culture has been part of Viêtnam for more than 2,000 years. When the country was freed from the colonial yoke of the French Republic, the Viêtnamese-Chinese, known among the Viêtnamese as Hoa, made up a large number of the middle class, especially when it came to doing business.

In South Viêtnam, they were thought to have controlled up to 80 percent of the country's economy. When the country was run by the French, the Hoa sided with the colonial powers, which led to friction between Hoa and Viêtnamese. This was exacerbated when Saigon fell in 1975. The Communist government stripped many of the Hoa community of their wealth, causing many of them to flee overseas, sometimes legally, but more often illegally, in boats, thus the term 'Boat People' coined by the West.

When the country was partitioned after the French left, ethnic Chinese in North Viêtnam were initially more accepted than their counterparts in the South simply due to them being descendants of a nation that had already embraced Communism in 1949. However, their status was strained in

Teenage Years

the late 1960s amidst the war as Ho Chi Minh leaned more towards the Soviet Union's backing rather than China.

Also, most ethnic Chinese families were not citizens of Viêtnam. They had kept their Chinese passports, with the majority not interested in becoming citizens of another country.

A decade earlier, the South Viêtnamese government of President Ngo Dinh Diem had taken stricter measures including, in 1956, making all Viêtnam-born Chinese people citizens of the country whether they wanted to be or not. Yet, first-generation Hoa born in China were not allowed residential permits but still had to pay their full taxes.

Not only did a lot of the Chinese-Viêtnamese not assimilate, but they also purposefully kept themselves separate from the locals as they saw themselves as more cultured.

Thiêu was part of a Chinese ethnic minority called the Teo Cheow, who were from Guangdong, a south-eastern province in China. And he was far from rich. However, he did learn lessons about his heritage and about the cultural mash-up that made him of Chinese ethnicity, but with a Viêtnamese outlook on many aspects of his life.

Originally, Viêtnam had no written language. It soon adopted a version of the Chinese Hanzi, or character-based, alphabet, before adopting a Latin-based alphabet introduced by the French. As for China, Thiêu believes that culture was leading the world in many areas for a long time, but avarice got in the way.

"I find that when there is wealth to be created, Chinese people keep it all to themselves, which causes the country to get smaller and smaller in terms of wealth," Thiêu says. "I find with Western countries; they tend to grow wealth. China led the world a thousand years ago, but they became too greedy.

"It's like saying, 'I am great at kung fu, but I don't want to teach anyone. Just my son.' I then tell my son not to tell anyone.

A Packet of Cigarettes

Because I only tell my son, he might forget a couple of things. And when he tells his son, his son might forget a couple of things. Not only that, but the father also holds 10 per cent of that knowledge back even from his son because he wants to have the prestige of only knowing certain things. Slowly the knowledge dies. This is why there are sometimes issues with Chinese people in other countries. We don't fully assimilate. It's the same with wealth."

Chapter 3

Thi Tô

As time went by, and Thiêu grew into his new job, he knew that it would soon be time to settle down, find a wife and start a family. Unfortunately for him, Asian culture puts a lot of kudos in your family background – what do your parents do? What type of family stock are you from? How much wealth has your family accumulated? What is your trade? How educated are you? Thiêu, being from a modest background, didn't have much going for him in terms of finding a partner. It wasn't just a case of whether he would find a woman who would love him, but a family that would accept him for who he was.

Two doors down from the hairdressers was a herbalist store run by the Trúóng family. Among the Trúóng's brood of eight children was 17-year-old Thi Tô, or Tô as she was known to her family. She helped run the store with her father after her eldest brother died in a vehicle accident. As infrastructure was an issue in most Viêtnamese villages, there was no running water at the herbalist store, therefore they had to use the water that was pumped into the hairdressing salon where Thiêu worked. The businesses split the bill. It was because of this that Thiêu and Tô first met each other – Tô would arrive at the salon and turn on the water for her father's store.

Can they both remember when they first met?

"He saw me first!" Tô says with a laugh.

Thiêu has a vivid memory of first laying eyes on the teenage Tô.

"I remember that she was wearing pants," Thiêu says. "And the reason I remember was that she must have been going through a growth phase because the bottom of her pants was riding up her legs because she had outgrown them. It looked a bit weird.

"I asked her what she was doing. She said she was being a 'citizen'. The Viêtnamese language is translated a little bit differently, but what I was essentially asking her is 'What are you being?' She said, 'I'm being a good citizen.' She was making a joke. So, I said, 'I'd like to be a citizen, too'."

They had to be careful about how they were being judged when talking together, because in the early 1960s, young men and women could not talk freely due to the cultural norms of the time, so they would say things in passing.

Thiêu only worried he might tarnish Tô's reputation. If she was caught talking with a man, it would spread and it would damage her standing in the community, which is why they talked secretly.

Luckily for Thiêu, Tô was not interested in being in a relationship with a person who would have to meet certain expectations set by the culture and her family. It came back to the patriarchal nature of Asian cultures.

Being a patriarchal society means Viêtnamese men are usually first in line when it comes to important decisions being made within a family, with women having minimal input.

However, this institution is exacerbated for women who marry into a family. They are at the bottom of the pecking order and can stay there for some time, especially if their husband's older sisters, or sisters-in-law, or even more worryingly, the mother-in-law, doesn't like them. The fact that Thiêu had no parents and only one sister – who was far too busy looking after her own growing family – was a bonus to Tô. From Thiêu's perspective, it worked out for him because as he had started with very little, there was only one way to go – up.

"In Viêtnam, we like to have big families," says Tô. "As a Viêtnamese woman, you are walking into a new family. You leave your family when you get married. I liked the fact that Thiêu had no family. He didn't have any baggage that came with him. As a wife to the family, you join the in-laws and clan. But I never wanted to join a clan. My ideal man was not somebody from a big family. I knew I wasn't one of those people who would like to join a big clan with older sisters and sister in laws. There would be too many people and too many conflicts and relationships you had to manage."

Tô admitted that she was not particularly good at doing household chores. If she was to take the traditional marriage route, she would need to be good at sewing, cooking, cleaning – all these things to show how valuable she could be to the in-laws and their family. And if you were not good, then the family could be mean to you. She never felt she had those skills, so didn't want to be in the space where she had to deal with difficult relationships.

However, her parents were not very happy about her liking Thiêu. She remembers one of the first things she noticed about him was his height (he was six feet, which was tall for a Viêtnamese man) and that he didn't have a big family. She only cared about him. Other women were choosing husbands who had big families, lots of money – all the things where they could

A Packet of Cigarettes

lean on other people. Tô didn't mind having less money as long as she had her freedom. She was happy to give herself to him.

Before any of this could happen however, there would be a roadblock. Thiêu got conscripted into the South Viêtnamese army. This wouldn't be the first time it happened. Before he left, Tô wanted to give him something of value but was poor. She decided to give him a packet of cigarettes to remind him that she would be waiting for him. He spent a year in the army and then went AWOL. Because of this, he couldn't go back to the village where the hairdresser was located, so he went back to Soc Trang because the army would not look for him there. He spent an extra two years there as a hairdresser before he felt it was safe enough to come back to get Tô.

"Love and romance in Viêtnam are not like it is in the Western world," says Thiêu.

Tô had to trust him as she waited for him. Sometimes he would send her a letter when he was thinking of her. Sometimes, there were months on end when they wouldn't speak. Tô had to get on with her life.

There was a girl in Soc Trang who liked Thiêu; she was the youngest of the hair salon owner's family. She was a nice girl but not as attractive as Tô. She was shorter, but she took care of Thiêu and the business. She let Thiêu know she liked him and that his opinion was important to her. He would decide what they would eat during the day, then she would buy the food and bring it home. If Thiêu said he felt like having beef today, which was an expensive protein, she would accommodate him and the other members of the hairdressing team.

"I could have stayed with her because my promise to Tô wasn't a deep promise, and I did like her," he says. "I didn't commit to the salon owner's daughter because I thought they had the wrong values. Her mother made sure there was a distinction between her family and the workers. I knew this because how she served water. Her family drank rainwater that had been filtered a couple of times. Everyone else had to drank river water that had been through one filter process. To me, that shows the quality of the family, and I didn't want to be part of a family with those values."

There were a couple of hurdles along the way, but he was a believer in fate and destiny: if he was supposed to be with Tô, she would get him.

"In the end, it was a packet of cigarettes that won out and me wanting to be a citizen with her," Thiêu says, laughing.

When he arrived back in Tô's village, she came by to say hello while on the way to another village to do some shopping. It was then that she met Thiêu's sister. Thiêu had told his sister that he would like to marry Tô. However, for the fledgling romance to bloom, as is custom, Thiêu needed somebody to speak to Tô's parents on his behalf.

In Viêtnam, when you want to marry somebody, you get a matchmaker – an in-between person – to talk to the parents. Because he was an orphan, Thiêu didn't have the right to talk to them because he was not at their level in society. Usually, the groom's father would go and talk on your behalf. Although Thiêu didn't have a father, he still needed somebody older to talk as his proxy – even in working-class Viêtnam there were protocols to be obeyed.

It was decided that his sister was also not at the same level as Tô's parents, so she could not talk to them. His old boss at the hairdressers said he would act as the representative for Thiêu. He helped buy all the gifts that needed to be given – such as sweets, sometime gold and cash, too. It is all part of asking for her hand in marriage.

According to Tô, even though her parents were not happy, they had to accept it. Some relatives were unhappy, some

A Packet of Cigarettes

were okay. Her mother ended up happy although her father was still dubious.

"He was thinking, 'Hairdresser, doesn't make a lot of money'," says Tô. "They didn't know Thiêu's origin and roots. He was a bit flirtatious being a hairdresser. They saw him as a good-looking man in contact with women all day. He might cheat on her, they thought."

"My father-in-law had to be careful. He was a bit nervous to say yes," says Thiêu.

"She said yes though. She told them that she didn't care. She would do it on her own without any of their support if she had to. She does everything by herself. We had an engagement ceremony. At that time in Viêtnam, we were very poor. We did not have a lot of money. Hardly enough to buy rice. It was nothing fancy. Have some tea and something to eat. Not like the banquets we've had in Australia or the West."

In 1966, they got married.

Chapter 4

The Army

In 1963, Thiêu was first conscripted into the army. The world around him was about to get a lot more heated. US troops were starting to have an increased presence. What had started as a trickle of 900 'advisors' in 1959 had ramped up to 16,000 military personnel in 1963.

By the time Thiêu got married in 1966, there were 385,000 US troops in South Viêtnam. Up until 1963, the South Viêtnamese armed forces were static at 243,000 members. In that year, they started to conscript young men, and by the war's practical – not actual – end in 1973, there were 1.1 million South Viêtnamese servicemen and women on active duty.

Thiêu was open about his stance on the Viêtnam War and the major players in it. He was antiwar from the get-go, as were most of the South Viêtnamese people he knew. They were no friends of Communism, but they also didn't like the way the South was run. He saw them as two peas in a pod – elites looking after their own.

A Packet of Cigarettes

Thiêu was no friend of the United States either. He knows that President John Kennedy, his successor Lyndon Johnson, as well as one of the architects of the United States' Viêtnam policy, Secretary of Defence Robert McNamara, all claimed it was about stopping the spread of Communism and how it would have a domino effect on the region.

The thought that such a large portion of the world's population would turn to Communism in such an important part of the globe was of concern to a superpower that was already fighting a Cold War with the USSR. Thiêu was not convinced.

"In 1954, when the French left the south part of Viêtnam, they owed the US money," says Thiêu.

"But they couldn't pay them back. I think they gave control of South Viêtnam to the US as some sort of payment. That is why I think America was in Viêtnam."

While this assertion has never been proven, it is not hard to see how a villager from rural South Viêtnam would see the politics of the situation play out. Going from one colonial former superpower to a 'free' government that looks like it is under the influence of a current superpower – one that has little or no cultural similarities to the people – is not a long bow to draw when you have had a subsistence living all your life. It was no wonder Thiêu was disinterested in being involved in a conflict that would – in his eyes – only benefit the elite of the side that won.

To understand Thiêu's point of view, you have to understand his thoughts at the time. As mentioned earlier, when the North and South were divided in 1945, northern leader Ho Chi Minh was already planning to unify the country. And when it was unified, it would be under Communist ideals set out by Ho and his cohort.

In 1956, elections were going to be held in both the North and South to decide on a government to run a single country.

The Army

Unsurprising, neither side, supported by their proxies – the USSR in the North and United States in the South – trusted each other, so the idea was unofficially nixed by South Viêtnam. This was not acceptable to the North, and in 1959, a meeting of the North Viêtnamese politburo agreed to help the communist South Viêtnamese sympathisers – the Viet Cong – overthrow the government of Ngo Dinh Diem.

To do this, they went into neighbouring Laos with the aid of that country's Communist armed wing, the Pathet Lao (who, like the Viet Cong, would eventually be successful in taking over their country), and also infiltrated parts of northeast Cambodia to set up a supply run that would eventually be known as the Ho Chi Minh Trail.

By the early 1960s, the Viet Cong were making inroads into South Viêtnam and 1963 turned out to be a nadir for not only Thiêu in terms of where he was heading in life, but South Viêtnam itself. On November 1, South Viêtnamese president Ngo Dinh Diem and his close advisors – including brother Ngo Dinh Nhu – were killed in a United States-backed coup. This had a catastrophic effect on the country as it left a power vacuum and massive infighting among the various political factions.

It was an open invitation for the Viet Cong to cause havoc, which they started to do immediately. This, in turn, set off a set of events that would substantially increase the number of United States troops in the country. All pretence of these troops being 'advisors' was gone, they were now fighting a war. An undeclared war on the part of the United States as its Congress had never officially approved it.

Into this environment stepped Thiêu, who had been living a quiet life cutting peoples' hair in rural South Viêtnam. One day, the police came to his house – and many others in the village – and conscripted him into the army. As with a lot of Third

A Packet of Cigarettes

World countries, the South Viêtnamese armed forces had a loose structure compared to its First World counterparts. While the officers were usually career men, a large part of those charged with the defence of the nation were conscripts as opposed to volunteers. This led to a lot of men only being on board because they had to and not because they supported the war.

"There were two types of army," says Thiêu. "There was the army for those that decided to join as volunteers, then there were those of us who were forced to join. We were treated differently. If the police come to get you, then you have little choice in what you do."

He had three months' training then was sent to different places around the country. He was trained in telecommunications and was given the task of carrying the radio for the Americans because he was taller than most Viêtnamese men. He saw himself as a pack horse. The radio was 14kg. He also had a handgun, which he rarely used. Was he a good shot and does he remember killing anybody?

"I had a gun and thought I might have to fight in the front line," he says. "If you don't, you are in trouble. Our leaders usually were at the back hiding. I shot a lot of bullets, but I didn't shoot anyone. I was a terrible shot. That is honest. It was very hard to kill someone. It was very hard to see someone and shoot them."

Before long, Thiêu deserted. It was a simple escape. Thiêu applied for a 24-hour pass, got it, left the camp and didn't come back when the pass expired. However, he soon had a change of heart and went back.

"That first AWOL (absent without leave) took the army a while to know I was missing because it took a long time to do the paperwork," he says.

"In that time, I quickly went back before they initiated the process. Once back, they could tell I was not that interested but couldn't just let me go, so I agreed to join the local militia

The Army

where I lived. I chose to be the telecommunicator in the local area. However, I had to pay money to do that in order to get out of the army – it was a one-off payment. It was a bribe."

Once back at the village, he continued hairdressing. He was in that position from 1964 until 1966 when he got married. Then, in 1968 he was conscripted again.

Like his previous sojourn, it didn't last long. One of the key turning points in the Việtnam War was the Tet Offensive whereby the Viet Cong, North Việtnamese Army (NVA) and many Communist sleeper cells based in South Việtnam, initiated a co-ordinated attack on strategic targets all over South Việtnam, all at the same time. Tet is the Chinese Lunar Year, so nobody was expecting it as many South Việtnamese armed forces personnel were on leave.

Just before it happened, Thiêu deserted again and he and Tô decided to go to stay with an aunt who lived in a small village near Cambodia because by this time he was known in Soc Trang as someone who should have been in the army.

"When the Tet Offensive started, I was still in my hamlet, and I didn't think this was a good thing, so we thought we might go to Cambodia just across the border just for peace and the children" he says.

At the border village, Thiêu was lucky enough to get work with a sergeant he knew who owned a little hair salon. Thiêu was protected by the sergeant. He wouldn't sell Thiêu out to the authorities. The man had opened the salon for his wife, and Thiêu was the head hairdresser for that business.

"Then the sergeant left the village, so I had to find another job. I found a man who was quite prominent in the community and worked with him," says Thiêu.

"This guy had a room in his house, so I set up a hairdressing shop there. We divided the profits. I had to duck and hide under more prominent people who would protect me."

A Packet of Cigarettes

It was then he decided to sell up and go to Cambodia. However, due to the Tet Offensive, there was a huge influx of Viêtnamese into Cambodia, so that government closed its border.

"We were lucky we didn't get into Cambodia because of what happened later with Pol Pot," says Thiêu.

Thiêu and Tô's first daughter, Bich Nhi (Jennifer), was born in 1967, a year after he got married. After he left the army for a second time, his next daughter, Tuyet Nhi (Dianne), was born. Two more children, Nhut Tan (Christopher) and Tu Nhi (Joanne), would arrive over the next few years.

"We were living in a storage shed when Dianne was born," said Thiêu.

"There was fertiliser and manure and chemicals. Dianne was born in the worst conditions. The younger two were born in hospital. Dianne was a home birth, and we were under a 10pm-5am curfew. She was born at 5am. I had to go and carry a lantern and let the soldiers know quickly that I was a civilian and that my wife was having a baby. I had to get a midwife to make sure the baby was delivered properly."

Once Dianne was born, trying times were ahead, not only because Thiêu had two young children, but the war was having an impact on everyone and everything around them. Then a little luck came the Cao family's way – the government brought in a rule that everybody had to have ID. This helped Thiêu out in the short term.

Thiêu started taking photos for IDs and made some money. The was the first amount of money he made in his life for himself as opposed for someone else.

"Before that, you couldn't make much money," says Thiêu.

But now, he had a side business for himself as well as working as a hairdresser. He saw it as a good opportunity. That was his savings. Before that, he only made enough money to live day to day.

The Army

During this time, he found there was uncertainty and unrest in his daily life due to the war going on which affected his choices. He couldn't make decisions for his long-term future. He could only make decisions for day-to-day living and how to avoid being conscripted. He didn't want to go too far from where he was living because he felt he would lose the safety of the connection of the people he knew. He didn't have anybody around him, which is why he went back to where his sister was, the village of Hưng Hoàng.

If having two children in tow and having to look after a family made Thiêu think his army days were over, he was mistaken. In 1970, he got conscripted for a third time.

"I went to all the training but when they sent me to war, I just left and went home," he says.

"I was about an hour from being dropped into the front line to fight, but I just up and left."

By now, the army was so big, and the bureaucracy running it so poor, that nobody missed him. The militia thought he was part of the army, and the army thought he was part of the local militia because the uniforms were similar. He pretended he was in the local militia so he told the army he needed to go back home to get something. He never went back.

But it didn't stop there. When he was doing photo IDs, he got an ID done for himself and made himself 10 years older so that he was over the age of conscription, but he had to pay for the document itself. i.e. although he took the photo, the ID's information had to be procured illegally.

"However, before the ID was ready, more papers arrived, which meant I was about to be conscripted again for a fourth time," he says.

"My wife was trying to send the falsified papers to me so I could pick them up and then I would be okay. When I left the army, I didn't have the papers on me, so I was worried. I had

A Packet of Cigarettes

to go to the meeting point and get the papers. I managed to get the ID and was saved."

Tô had moved to Saigon with her older brother Hon Van (Happy Uncle). She had decided to leave the village because the only family she had there was her sister-in-law and she wanted to be closer to her larger, extended family, some of which had moved to the bigger city.

She had money that the family had saved from the ID photos, so she and her brother opened up a white goods store that also had TVs, radios and similar items.

When she made the move, the war was going on in the countryside, with the odd incursion into the city. These were mainly infiltrators who were trying to seek an advantage for their comrades in the NVA and Viet Cong who were moving supplies along the Ho Chi Minh Trail. The North Viêtnamese knew the key to victory was the taking of Saigon – the biggest stronghold for the South Viêtnamese government.

Meanwhile, life continued for the Cao family. They had jobs to do and schools to attend. Even with the war going on around them, Thiêu was more concerned about providing for his family than who was running the country. Ever the entrepreneur, having survived by his wits and common sense for most of his life, he set about earning a living.

There were no openings for a hairdresser in Saigon, so he applied for a job in a poultry factory – nothing too cerebral, but enough to feed and clothe his young family in uncertain times. While he was waiting for the word to come through about the factory job, he set about building a cart to sell vegetables and fruit along the roadside. Just as he finished the cart, word came through that he had got the job at the poultry factory.

"But I had the cart, so I didn't know what to do with it," says Thiêu.

The Army

"It just so happened that the man who had taken me to get my falsified papers visited me. He was down on his luck, so I gave him the cart and gave him some money for helping me. He ended up selling durian while I went and worked in the factory."

Because providing food was an essential service, getting the job at the poultry factory had other advantages other than helping Thiêu provide for his family – it gave him cover from the authorities.

"Because the factory is big and affiliated with some big wigs, they protected us," he says.

"I was not going to be hassled. I had papers if I really needed them but once I started working there, the authorities left me alone."

His concern was that if he went out in the public too often, they might notice him, which is why working somewhere where he wasn't on the street all day was important – even though the false papers would pass official scrutiny. He ended up working there from 1972-1975 and operated the hatching machine.

During that time, their third child, Nhut Tan (Chris), was born. Tô and her brother, Happy Uncle, ran the white goods store for a while, which enabled them to buy a house. Once they were established in the house, it was decided that Thiêu would have the front room and use it as a sewing machine repair shop as well as working in the poultry plant.

Several years before the French had left Viêtnam, they had built a sewing machine factory. By 1975, the factory had burned down, but there were still plenty of its products being used throughout the city. This is where Thiêu's expertise kicked in as he could utilise parts from broken machines to repair machines that would help those who were running their own cotton industries from the back allies and front porches of their homes.

However, life was about to take a turn for the worse.

Chapter 5

The Fall of Saigon

On April 30th, 1975, the city of Saigon fell to the forces of the Peoples' Army of Viêtnam (PANV) and their southern allies, the Viêt Công. The fate of the South had been sealed three years earlier during the Paris Peace Accords of 1972, where US President Richard Nixon agreed to withdraw all US troops from the country. The quid pro quo was that all fighting would stop, and the countries would go back to their 1954 demarcation line of the 17th Parallel.

The North had no intention of sticking to the accords, because no sooner had the US started to depart, the hostilities started again. Nixon did send in the US air force in Operation Linebacker, which initially stopped the reinvasion. However, with a US presidential election due, an oil crisis and its associated looming recession – as well as the war becoming more unpopular at home – the US people were in no mood for more of its men to die in a war that many already considered not only lost, but none of its business.

The Fall of Saigon

The South itself was led by a corrupt government, and even more corrupt armed forces leadership. The population, while not keen for a Communist takeover, was unwilling to lay down their lives for a bureaucracy that only had its own self-interest at heart.

Saigon itself had remained largely unscathed during the war. Overall, it was business as usual on the streets. Life was not easy, but it was relatively safe.

"There were no bombs or anything like that," says Thiêu. "You could stay in a village 2km from Saigon and that is where the Communists were. You just didn't go out there."

Thiêu has vivid memories of the fall of Saigon. It was a day he will never forget, but also, he knew within a month that he would leave the country.

"Our house was right next to a bridge and there was an army watch tower on the bridge," he says. "We thought we might get caught in collateral damage as the Communists entered the city."

His second eldest daughter, Dianne, also remembers the day vividly. The then six-year-old knew something big was happening and knew that it couldn't be good.

"On that day, I thought we stayed in the house for a while," she says.

"I couldn't get anywhere I was so scared. Mum and Dad had given us a pack that included our address and date of birth on it and our parent's names in case we got lost. We were supposed to go to Happy Uncle's house, who lived further away from the bridge and near a hospital."

"If anything happened, then we would be near the hospital and admission would be easier. Dad didn't want to leave our house in case some people tried to loot it. He wanted to maintain his business and possessions. I remember starting the journey but never making it. It must have been the day of the

A Packet of Cigarettes

fall, and everybody was there. There were crowds everywhere. Mum gave us the equivalent of AUD$10 and told us which army person to find if we got lost – those in camouflage were South Viêtnamese, those in green were North Viêtnamese. We never quite made it and went back home due to the crowds."

Chapter 6

Life Under Communism

Once the South had surrendered, a sort of calm descended on the city. The rumours of mass reprisals failed to emerge, although some of South Viêtnam's government officials and army personnel did end up being killed and some military officers would spend the best part of a decade being 're-educated'. Once the last of the US helicopters had left, the reality of the situation sunk in.

"I remember crying in the morning about a week after the fall," says Thiêu.

"They closed the university of law and then I knew all our freedom was gone. I thought justice and righteousness were gone and it was about to become the law of the jungle. Whoever had the gun had the most say. The life of my children was never going to be the same. It was going to be an unfairness in the society that we were about to inherit.

"My next thought was at least there was no more war and there was a leader in the country and there was going to be

A Packet of Cigarettes

some sort of person in charge. We had to accept the current situation."

Once Thiêu was resigned to the fact he would be living under Communist rule, he renovated the house because he thought that was going to be his lot in life and he would raise his children the best he could. However, he didn't like his situation and thoughts of leaving the country started ruminating in his mind.

Soon after the fall, the Communist regime changed Saigon's name to Ho Chi Minh City in honour of the party's venerated leader who had passed away in 1969, failing to the see the fulfilment of his dream – a united Viêtnam. Thiêu knew that life under Communism was going to be a lot harder than under the South Viêtnamese government.

While corruption among the bureaucracy in the South was rife, at least there were freedoms that would no longer apply under the new government. It didn't take long for the Communist's own form of bureaucracy to rear its ugly head. Thiêu knew things would only get worse.

He quickly realised how volatile things had become in the recently united country. For example, the Communist regime kept on changing the money. People were constantly having to trade in their old money for new money and the new money was always severely devalued. A person could give the Communist-run bank 100,000 dong and they would give you 500 back. Thiêu remembers one day going to a money exchange, giving them 200 dong, and they gave him 1 Viêt Công dong back.

"Whatever money you have in the bank – whether it be 1 million dong or 1,000 – they'd give you the same figure," he says.

"When you wanted to withdraw money, you had to apply to do so. And you had to have a reason for withdrawing the money. The maximum you could take out in a day was 200 dong.

Life Under Communism

"I realised that the system was terrible. They would take your money away from you in a way that is legal under their system. Communists are like that. I believe the Communists kept us so busy with so many activities and causing stress and confusion, that you don't have the will or free thought to fight them. You're busy trying to make it through the day; you have no time for anything else. You can't have any constructive thoughts to go against them."

Tô remembers bad things happening to previously wealthy South Viêtnamese.

She said her family was lucky because they did not have a lot of money, so the authorities left them alone. The ones with money, if the government liked their house, they would stay in the house. They would live in the bottom level, and they would let the owners live in the top level. They wouldn't kick them out, but it was not a comfortable existence. When the owner would come and go from the premises, they had to tell the Communists why they were leaving and where they were going. Tô says she knew of a person who was killed because he had too much money and they wanted to take it, and he tried to stop them.

"In the Communist era, you did not make much money and if you made too much you were in trouble," says Thiêu.

"You made enough to live. If you were too poor you had trouble finding enough to eat, and if you were too rich you were in trouble with authorities. If you were in the middle not much changed under Communists. Even now if you go back to Viêtnam, you have just enough money to spend. If you become a millionaire, you will see trouble soon."

Many South Viêtnamese soldiers and intellectuals were sent to re-education camps after the war. While there were no massacres, life under Communism was hard. The new government moved almost one million people out of Saigon, a large number of which had been refugees from the countryside. Now unified, there was no need to have so many people in the city where unemployment was rife. The government needed people out in the fields getting food production up and running again.

The world was going through a recession as the oil crisis took hold, while Viêtnam itself was having difficulties with its former allies – China and Cambodia. China was annoyed that its proxy was on friendly terms with the USSR. While all three countries were founded on Communist ideals, that is where similarities ended. China didn't like the idea of the USSR having any impact or influence of what it considered its own back yard.

As the war had continued, the North Viêtnamese had leaned heavily on the USSR for aid and military support. This angered China because by the end of the war, 1,100 of its soldiers had been killed in support of the PARV and Viet Cong, while the USSR had lost just 16 'advisors'.

Meanwhile, on the western border, any influence that Viêtnam thought it had on Cambodia soon evaporated after Pol Pot, also known as Brother Number One among his cronies, took over. He immediately started cleansing the country of its intelligentsia – and then some – with between 1-3 million people dying in the Killing Fields.

It would eventually lead to Viêtnam invading Cambodia and ousting Pot and his murderous regime. This in turn would lead to China invading Viêtnam in what would later be described as a border skirmish between the two nations. This wariness is still in place four decades later.

None of this had an immediate effect on Thiêu or his family. They were too worried about making ends meet. And with the way things were going with their business, the situation might have to get worse before it got better.

Life Under Communism

"When the Communists took over, they saw the burned sewing machine factory and all the spare parts around it as belonging to them," says Thiêu.

"We continued to fix the old sewing machines and sold them to the North Viêtnamese. At the shop, we still had stock, but we soon ran out."

People also had to prioritise their spending to stay under the radar of the Communist authorities. Thiêu remembers people selling family items so they could have money to buy food but didn't want too much money as it would arouse suspicion.

What sort of life did he think the children might have if they stayed?

"With the children, I realised the difficulty wasn't just financial, but about direction and how to guide them and give them a career path," he says.

"A university education was out of our reach. We were not members of the Communist Party, and at the time, intellectuals were not well thought of. At best, I thought I might be able to give them a trade and help them make a living."

For example, he thought Jennifer could be a photographer. He had some experience with his ID photo side hustle. In Saigon and the surrounding countryside, there were still French boarding schools for girls. They would not allow male photographers on site, but they would allow a young lady.

He says he knew how to outsmart the Communists, but his main concern was that his children's generation would not know how to deal with them. He wanted to leave Viêtnam for their sake.

Chapter 7

The Boat

Both Thiêu, and Happy Uncle, knew Communism was not going to benefit the family. There was no incentive to work or save under such a regime. As mentioned, you couldn't earn too much money, or you would come to the attention of the authorities. And if you earned just enough to have a subsistent living – well, that was hardly living at all. The family was more ambitious than that.

It was then that they had the idea of buying a fishing boat. Not because they thought it would be a great living, but because it would give them a means to escape the country. However, they had to be smart about it. Buying the boat and then leaving straight away was not an option. Not because they didn't want to – there were a couple of more immediate problems; nobody knew how to fish, and nobody knew how to navigate a boat.

It was Happy Uncle's idea to get the boat, but he couldn't work on it because he was not used to manual labour. Thiêu came from the country so knew a lot about hard labour.

The Boat

"My mother-in-law pointed out that Happy Uncle couldn't do the work, so she said I should do it. I did the fishing and left the chicken factory behind," says Thiêu.

"My wife took over the sewing machine job even though a lot of the work had dried up. While my wife knew how to fix a radio, she could not fix sewing machines. She sold spare parts for the sewing machine and got what she could. She didn't know about the pricing, but she made enough to feed the children."

Thiêu moved to the seaside village of Bac Lieu where the boat was moored and set about learning how to become a fisherman. With no experience in how to work a boat, at first, the family hired people to help them run the vessel as fishing in Viêtnam can be a dangerous affair due to the tides and various seasonal variations in the tropics. You can leave the dock on a calm, clear day, but the weather can change in an instant, especially during typhoon season. In the mid-1970s, weather reports in Viêtnam were unreliable. Thiêu hired several experienced fishermen to show him the ropes.

The boat was about 22 metres long and they needed to have seven to eight people working on it. There was nothing automated about fishing. They used manpower and nets. There was no air conditioning or freezer. They had 50kg blocks of ice to keep the fish fresh and used rice husks to cover the ice to insulate it. It would last seven to eight days, which was the length of each voyage.

"We didn't go deep water fishing. We caught what we could and sorted them into various fish species and took them to the market. We sold a lot of fish," says Thiêu.

After about 12 months, Thiêu started to become efficient in the ins and outs of how to run a boat. He then put the second part of his plan into motion – start bringing family members on board as crew so that when they left, there were enough proficient sailors.

A Packet of Cigarettes

Again, Thiêu had to be smart. Making all his current crew redundant at once in favour of his own family would arouse suspicion. Replacing them over time, would not only allay those suspicions, but would make sense to those in the village and to the authorities – most families in Viêtnam who had a business would employ their relatives and/or friends before strangers.

Family members mainly consisted of Tô's relatives – such as cousins – people in their late teens and young men. All the hard, laborious work that Thiêu had carried out since his early teens paid off as fishing was a physically intensive job that required strength, endurance and mental toughness. All of which Thiêu had.

While Thiêu takes credit for getting everybody up to speed on how to work a fishing boat, he says Happy Uncle was the one responsible for making sure that the right strategies were put in place for when they were ready to leave.

"My brother had all the connections," says Tô. "He knew how to strategise and get things together. Thiêu had to action it."

"Happy Uncle was the oldest son in my wife's family, so he took charge of a lot of things," says Thiêu.

"It is a role you step into. If you are the eldest son, you don't have a choice. His older brother died in a motorcycle accident; Happy Uncle stood up because he was second in line. Whenever these major things happen, it is usually the father planning with the son. My father-in-law would plan with him and all the other brothers. They became senior members of the family, but Happy Uncle was the head."

Having secrets wasn't ideal and trying to keep quiet about what the family was planning was hard. All it would take was an accidental slip of the tongue or saying something at the wrong time in front of the wrong company, and the boat would be confiscated and the family stuck in Viêtnam.

The Boat

Thiêu, his father-in-law and Happy Uncle decided to keep the leaving date among only senior members of the family. This was hard when it came to planning for day-to-day life. They had a certain time frame to work to but had to pretend to plan for events they knew would never happen as they would be long gone.

It was under these conditions that Thiêu decided to tell his sister of what he was planning. He was apprehensive about telling her, not because he didn't want her to come with him – it was the opposite, he really wanted her on board – it was more about who he didn't want to invite.

"I would not allow her husband to come because he was not a very good man," says Thiêu.

"He had a second wife. He made a lot of bad decisions, and I did not like him. He had too many children with his other wife. You can't trust a man like that. We didn't have any legal documents. We only live by family way – trust. What we have together, we have together."

His sister turned down his offer because she wanted to stay with her husband and didn't want her children separated from their father. She kept Thiêu's offer to herself and never told anyone.

While Thiêu was sad about her decision, it was her choice to make, and he never held it against her. In later years, when the family had settled in Australia, he would return to Viêtnam and visit her often. Eventually, four of her children would settle in Australia with Thiêu's help.

However, long before he had even seen Australia, he had bigger things to worry about. While the family was slowly starting to look the part – of real fishermen – the venture was almost over before it began.

Chapter 8

Lost at Sea

FISHING CAN BE A DANGEROUS AFFAIR, not just in Viêtnam but all around the world. The days of 24/7 up-to-the-minute weather reports were still not common in western countries, let alone in a third-world country like Viêtnam in the 1970s.

While the wet and dry seasons would allow some predictability, it was impossible to foresee what the weather might be doing three or four hours into the future – let alone the following day.

And this became an issue for Thiêu a year into his fishing adventure. One day, after 10 days of fishing, they were heading home. Just as they reached the heads of the bay from which the boat had been launched, the engine quit, and they were adrift. This in itself was not disastrous. However, the ensuing storm that arrived not long after was, which in turn was compounded when the two anchors that they had put out to stop them drifting, snapped.

Lost at Sea

Thiêu knew they were in trouble after the anchors were gone, not because of they were drifting aimlessly, but because of the captain's reaction.

"The captain sat down and started to cry. That was not a good sign," says Thiêu.

"We thought we would wait for a bigger boat to come out and hook us in and tow us to land. But there was no-one around because of the storm. Once the anchors failed, we started drifting. There was a small island at the heads where there were Communist soldiers. We tried to make a signal to get them to help, but no one came. I think they were lazy."

After a few hours, they could still see an island but were now a long way from home. Two of Tô's cousins on board came up with the idea of swimming to the land. However, Thiêu knew that distances could be deceptive. He was concerned that they might not make it, but they were determined to give it a try.

Seeing that they would not be deterred, he tried to give them some practical advice. On board was a long, thick malleable tube that was hollow, and also an empty petrol container. Thiêu told them to clean the tube. They filled the tube with water and tied both sides so they would have fresh water when they got onto land.

"The petrol container would be the buoy, and the tube would be the water," he says. "It was a 200-litre tank that would help them float.

"I gave them strategies to survive if they were to make it to the island. There was going to be fruit to eat and fish to hunt, which was okay but fresh water would be hard to get. This water was going to help them survive. The tank would help them to shore. They would need to sterilise the water first and wrap the tube around the tank. I told them I was going to go down with the boat. I had no desire to swim. If the boat didn't make it home, neither would I."

A Packet of Cigarettes

By the time everything was ready, the brothers changed their mind because they could see that they had drifted too far from the island, plus it was getting hard to see in the night. While the boat itself was in a reasonable condition, there were not many provisions for survival. There was the ice they used to keep the fish cool, which could be melted, as well as some rice.

They decided to use these two provisions to make congee, which would make the supplies last longer. It was a watery concoction, but one that would keep hunger pangs at bay.

It was only due to luck that they managed to survive. Before setting out on every trip, Thiêu always took a couple of hacksaw blades with him, which they used to cut the ice and do other minor tasks. For some inexplicable reason, Thiêu had decided to take a dozen blades for this trip.

Thiêu didn't know why the boat had broken down because he knew nothing of engines. He asked the captain, and he explained that there was something wrong with the cogs in the gears in the engine – they were broken. Because of Communism, Viêtnam didn't import any new parts from overseas, so much like the sewing machine business, they used old parts that were a bit hit and miss in terms of being in proper working order.

"I came up with the idea of using the hacksaw blades together to cut out a new cog from a spare piece of metal we had on board. I had a look at the engine and told the crew that if we committed ourselves to fixing it, and if we did it together, it would work. Everybody said yes, and we started to fix it. We started sawing at 10am one day, until 4am the next morning to make a new cog to make sure it worked. It took us 16 hours to fix the engine. We put the new part into the engine, and it worked," said Thiêu triumphantly.

By the time the part was ready to be implanted into the engine, they figured they had drifted a long way and were closer to the shores of Thailand than Viêtnam; not a place many Viêtnamese fishermen wanted to be as Thailand was a haven for pirates.

When they turned the engine on, they powered it up very slowly, so it didn't destroy the new part. This allowed the cog to slowly wear in and they started heading back to Viêtnam. Everyone's relief was palpable.

"I said, 'Only celebrate when we get near to Viêtnam'," he says.

"We weren't looking for our port, we just wanted to go home and didn't care what port we were in. We used sticks to measure the depth of the water to make sure we didn't run aground. We could see rubbish coming out from the mainland, so we followed the rubbish. We had a compass, but we didn't know where we were. We found some fishermen and told them we were lost, and we were from Bac Lieu. We ended up at a place called Nam Can."

When they got on land, they all fell asleep because they were so tired. They had over a ton of fish onboard. The next day it was low tide, and the boat was on dry land.

But the drama didn't end there. Because the whole country was now on a subsistence living, this meant that nobody in the new village was keen to do them any favours, so they had to think on their feet to get enough funds to refloat the boat and get other provisions.

"We had to sell everything we could to get cash," Thiêu says.

"Our watches, radio – everything we had. We needed to buy salt to make salty fish so we could sell the fish because there was a market in the village. Then we had to buy oil to get the engine running. We had to buy a rope from someone in the village. With the rope, we dragged the boat out when high tide came in."

A Packet of Cigarettes

Meanwhile, back in Bac Lieu, where the rest of the family were waiting. Tô and the rest of the village had no idea where the fishermen were. They were supposed to come back after 10 days. The fact that they were already three days overdue meant they assumed they were lost at sea. They had seen the storm and thought the worst. They didn't know whether the crew had survived or not but knew that the outcome couldn't have been good.

Tô's father would wait on the pier and ask other people on boats if they had seen them. They thought they had perished. Thiêu sent one of the younger cousins by land with some money from Nam Can to let everybody else know they were okay and not to worry.

The cousin got home before the crew did. They knew the people at Bac Lieu would be worried sick.

Chapter 9

Leaving – 1977

Just over 200km north of Bac Lieu, was the border of Cambodia. Just as the NVA and Viêt Công were making the final assault on South Viêtnam, the military arm of the Cambodian Communist Party, the Khmer Rouge, were fighting the nationalist US-backed forces of the Cambodian government.

The capital of Cambodia, Phnom Penh, was overrun by Communist forces on April 17th, 1975, 13 days before Saigon fell to the Viet Cong and NVA. While both countries soon had similar political regimes, it was far from a happy relationship.

Cambodia, under the leadership of megalomaniac Pol Pot, was concerned that Viêtnam would try and start up some sort of Pan French Indochina federation – including Laos – whereby Viêtnam would be at the head of the table, to whom the two smaller nations would pledge fealty. This was not something that Pol Pot or his cronies were willing to endure.

A Packet of Cigarettes

After 1975, while there was underlying tension between both governments, there was little in the way of conflict. However, by April 1977, the relationship had broken down to such to extent that Khmer Rouge soldiers invaded Viêtnam. It was in this environment, and due to not wanting to live under Communist rule, that in late 1977, the Cao and Trúóng families decided it was time to leave.

By now, Thiêu had garnered enough trust with his wife's family that he was part of the inner circle of decision makers. While he did defer a lot of the decisions to his father-in-law – as Viêtnamese/Chinese custom dictated – he was still a considered voice. Thiêu, his father-in-law and Happy Uncle were at loggerheads initially about when to leave.

Both Thiêu and Happy Uncle knew that the time was right to leave, but the father-in-law was getting antsy – he wanted to leave too but thought that the stakes might be too high. He thought it was too risky for many reasons – the Communists might capture them, or if they made it into international waters, Thai pirates might take all their possessions or sink the boat. Then there was the seaworthiness of the boat itself, even though it has recently managed to navigate not only being lost at sea, but a storm, too.

Eventually, Thiêu's father-in-law relented and agreed they needed to leave. However, their first attempt was not successful. Before they even left shore, they failed due to a miscommunication.

The initial plan was that Thiêu was going to pilot the boat. His father-in-law had a good friend, and they wanted their families to go together. The other family had organised the people onshore who were going to taxi the families out to the boat.

Between them, both families paid 15 ounces of gold – 7.5 ounces each. That attempt failed because the family friend who was supposed to organised it got the day wrong. The men he

Leaving – 1977

had paid to pick people up from the shore and take them to the boat didn't appear because they thought it was happening two days later, which is what had been communicated to them.

"The boat was out in the harbour but the little boats that were supposed to take the families out there, and the crew, couldn't be found," says Thiêu. "So, my mother-in-law and father-in-law went home not too sure if it was an omen of things to come."

Wasn't the family worried that somebody might sell them out to the Communists?

"Not really," confirmed Thiêu.

The family were very tight lipped about who they told. Also, any chances of repercussions for those left behind were slim. Not because the authorities were of a reconciliatory disposition, but simply because they had no idea who was related to whom.

While their disappearance might be noted by their neighbours, the authorities wouldn't even know who they were as no census had been taken. That didn't mean if they were caught leaving, they wouldn't be in trouble. All the adults would have gone to re-education camps for as long as would take them to get indoctrinated, while the children would have to fend for themselves. It wasn't quite as harsh as some totalitarian regimes where executions were a matter of course, but there was enough disincentive there that they wanted to make the break as clean as possible.

"The discussions you have with the people who leave or don't leave is not the fear of retribution, it is the fear of being stopped," says Thiêu. "If your family knows you are going, but they don't want to go, they can tell authorities because they want you to stay."

Thiêu would canvas certain people within the family first to see if they wanted to go. For example, he spoke to those closest to him first, like his sister. He would ask a person if

A Packet of Cigarettes

they wanted to stay or go. Thiêu would have a 'what if?' type of conversation, as opposed to a 'this is what we are doing, are you in or out?' type of talk. He kept his cards close to his chest so those that weren't interested would just think it was a case of 'chewing the fat'.

"Most people wanted to leave. However, it is a very hard and personal decision to decide to go," says Thiêu.

"The reason my sister didn't want to leave was because I told her that I would only take her because she was my sister, and there was only a limited number of people that could fit on the boat. I offered her and her single children a place on the boat, but not her married children or husband. For her, it was an emotional decision. She couldn't rip the family apart. She decided to stay."

When they finally left, there were 27 people on the boat – 17 members of the Cao and Trúong clans and the other family who had tried to arrange the first attempt at leaving.

On the day they left, Thiêu remembers it was a low tide.

"I felt heavy in my heart because it was the biggest decision of my life," he says.

"Up until then, I hadn't made many big decisions. I had the life of my family in my hands – live or die. It was a very tough decision. In the days leading up to the departure, I hardly slept and was anxious and worried."

Tô was more circumspect and practical.

"You get beyond fear because you hope that the steps that you have taken will be fine," she says.

"You only focus on your decision and your step. My role was to make sure the family got to the boat on time. I had to make sure everything I had planned is done right. The bigger worry was to make sure everything else fell into place."

The first attempt to leave had failed due to miscommunication. It was different this time around. To allay suspicion, they

Leaving – 1977

decided that they would leave via small groups at a little beach near the village. They would be rowed out to the boat instead of going to the port – 27 people all arriving at once on the port to go on a boat would make even the most disinterested communist official take notice.

One of the more important aspects of leaving was making sure the children would not draw attention to authorities. This is why the early morning was chosen as a lot of the younger kids were half or fully asleep and therefore not aware what was going on. As long as they were snuggled up tight with an adult, they seemed okay. Eight of the kids were under 10, but it was the toddlers that caused most of the concern in case they awoke crying. Just to make sure, some of them were given antihistamines, so they would fall asleep.

To make things comfortable for the trip, Thiêu made a pseudo cabin where the ice boxes should have been. Although the chances of being stopped when leaving were minimal, he didn't want to take any chances. He decided that once the cabin was made and there was enough ventilation, it would be a good idea to put some ice over it, so it still looked like a fishing boat.

"Because I had done the trip many times, they recognised me. In preparation for leaving, I went out the day before," he says.

"Just before we came into port, I shut one of the cylinders down on the engine which meant it was only running on three cylinders. You can really hear a difference in the motor when you do that. It makes a racket. As I went past the authorities on the dock, they looked at me because they could tell something was wrong with the boat. I said to them that there was an issue with the engine, and I needed to get it fixed.

"This was done so that when we left the next day and we saw them sitting by the dock, they would be so interested in the fact that I got the engine going again, that they wouldn't even think to do a random stop on us. It worked. When I picked up the people the following morning, I had put the cylinder in working order. As we left, I waved to them and yelled at them that the boat was now working okay."

Thiêu also decided to leave early in the morning because the tide was low. This meant that in the off-chance soldiers did want to inspect the boat, they would have to walk across the mud flats. If the tide had been high, they could have rowed across, which would have been much easier

Chapter 10

At Sea

BEING A FORWARD THINKER, Thiêu knew that there were dangers at sea as well as on land – pirates. If they wanted to, the group could have headed straight for Thailand, which was a 24-hour trip. However, Thailand was where most of the pirates came from.

They were not pirates in the traditional sense. Most were Thai fisherman, who were armed and would fleece the unarmed refugees of their most valuable possessions. Some people were killed, but Thiêu knew they mostly wanted their valuables – gold and diamonds – that most of the travellers had hidden on the boat or their person.

"I learned in the army how to read a map and use a compass," he says.

"That is why I was comfortable heading out to the middle of the ocean and then back to land. It was a less direct route, but safer. When you are in international waters, local laws don't matter. The pirates have guns and machetes. They also have bigger boats, and they can ram you. A lot of people ran into pirates, especially if they went the direct route."

Taking the less direct route to Malaysia would mean they would be at sea for 48 hours. Taking even the best precautions wouldn't mean the trip would be smooth. And it wasn't.

Once out at sea, and with his navigation skills coming to the fore, it was modern technology that gave Thiêu his first hint there was trouble – a blip on the boat's rudimentary radar. As time wore on, he noticed that the blip was getting closer. He had a decision to make. He could try and out run the other vessel, but risk the engine blowing up, which would leave them stranded.

Alternatively, he could also just keep going at the pace they were going. He could also tell by the radar that no land was nearby, and that it would take the other boat about two hours to catch them.

He chose a third option. Head towards the boat.

"In Viêtnamese, we have a saying, 'Thieves are afraid of beggars'," he says.

"Thieves are only after people with money. So, when you start heading towards them, what you are telling them is that we are needier than you. They think that we are poor."

Soon enough, the boat caught up with them. Thiêu was on the offensive straight away and asked for food and told them that his boat's engine was about to seize. He had also been taught a couple of tricks by fisherman he had worked with when he bought the boat. The first was never have your vessel parallel with the other ship.

"You try and face them with the front of your boat into the side of theirs if possible because you could jack knife them if you had to," he says. "You also never turn your engine off because you can manoeuvre a lot quicker than them. It takes them longer to move around you."

At Sea

Thiêu told all the other passengers what he was going to do and to let him do all the communicating. And it was communication of sorts because the Thai 'fishermen' couldn't speak Viêtnamese and Thiêu couldn't speak Thai. He told them that they were lost and hungry.

While Thiêu was communicating with the Thai captain, he told his co-captain to move the boat forward and backward and not to stand still. He even doubled down to make out that they were truly in a perilous predicament.

"I had a basket that I tied to a rope and threw it over to them and pointed at their fish. They threw some fish back," he says.

At one point, one of the Thai crew members jumped on board the vessel to check everything out. They wanted to have a look to see if Thiêu was telling the truth.

"The guy who came over to our boat had a look around," says Thiêu.

"We looked like we were mainly women and kids and very poor and didn't have much. The other family had gold strapped to their body. They were worried that they might start searching us and they would have found something. But I think because I took the attack to them, they left us alone. Although I did trade them some of our ice for their fish."

Chapter 11

Arrival

ALTHOUGH THE CAO-TRÚỒNG FAMILY were not the first Viêtnamcsc boat people to leave the country, they were part of the first wave. When they left, it was October 1977, Communists had been in charge of Viêtnam for just over two years. Pol Pot's murderous regime in Cambodia – the Killing Fields – was well underway, and the Cold War was still ongoing.

Ten years before, there had been Communist insurgencies in surrounding countries including Malaysia and Indonesia. There was a lot of suspicion between the differing nations, which meant refugees from those countries that had open conflict – such as Viêtnam and Cambodia – were not welcome in most neighbouring countries.

The UN was running most refugee programs, so at a political level, there was a moral obligation for these countries to help out. Most would never dream of taking in refugees permanently, but there was an understanding that any genuine

Arrival

refugees that landed on the shores of the more democratic South-east Asian countries would eventually be settled in first-world countries such as Canada, the US, New Zealand and Australia.

This didn't mean the host countries would not make it as difficult as possible for the refugees to land. Malaysia was no exception as Thiêu was about to find out. It would also mean he would take dramatic steps to make sure that once they arrived, they couldn't be sent back.

Thiêu knew he was approaching land when he saw bird life and rubbish in the water. He also could tell by the compass that it had to be Malaysia. They were too far south for it to be Thailand and too far north for it to be Indonesia. Also, they were heading west, so it was the only country it could be.

He followed a rubbish line and soon ran into a Malaysian patrol boat.

"They were officials," says Thiêu. "I asked them about the UN, and they said there was no UN facilities nearby.

"They acted like they want to help us, but I could tell that they didn't really want to. They asked if we have petrol, oil, food and all that stuff. I said we did. They pointed to an island that was way in the distance, and they said that was where the UN was, and we had to go there. They said if we stayed where we were, there might be pirates and robbers turning up. We spoke in Chinese."

Thiêu could barely make out the island in the distance and knew it was too far for his boat to go. He also knew he couldn't fight the authorities so pretended to agree with them and started heading towards the island. Slowly. As soon at the patrol was out of sight, he started headed southwest again. Towards the shore.

"We were such a small boat; we didn't have the ability to make it to the island," he says.

A Packet of Cigarettes

"The boat would be dead before any of that stuff happened. We were near land, so I wasn't going to go anywhere else. Later on, when we landed, I spoke to people about the island, and they said the island was deserted and there was no UN facility there."

Once they reached the coastline, they followed it, looking for an opportunity to land. More importantly, they were looking for an elusive UN facility. Before they left, they had heard there was such a camp, and they needed to reach it because they didn't want to be at the mercy of the Malaysian authorities. Thiêu also felt that if he stayed near the coastline and something bad happened, they could abandon ship. While the terrain could be hostile, it would be better than being stuck on a boat in the middle of the ocean.

"We went along until we found houses and villages," says Thiêu.

"I sent two of the younger men who had language skills – my youngest brother-in-law could speak a little bit of English and a couple of others could speak Mandarin – and they scouted around."

They found a man of Chinese descent by knocking on his door. Because they shared Chinese ancestry, he helped them. He told them that they couldn't stay at the village because he would get in trouble with the authorities and might even end up in jail for helping them.

He told them to go along the coast, past a couple of coconut farms, and they would soon come across the UN compound. Thiêu's boat headed that way and sure enough, they soon spotted a huge fishing boat near to where they had to go. He recognised the mast as someone from Viêtnam. A man swam out to them.

"He looked pretty tired but when he got on board, he gave us some good information," says Thiêu.

Arrival

"He told us that we were in the right place, but the best thing to do was make sure the boat was no longer seaworthy. If the boat is in good condition, they'll send you back out to sea because the Malaysian government didn't want to take people in because it was a burden for them to do so. They may do it for humanitarian reasons, but if they think you are okay, and your boat is okay, they'll send you back out to sea again. This was Malaysia's position. They don't want to facilitate the arrival of refugees, but they won't turn you away if you are in trouble."

Thiêu laughed when he told this part of the story, because the hardest thing to do was make a boat seaworthy. Being told – in order to survive – you need to make the boat unseaworthy, is something that is easy to do.

"We drilled holes in the boat to make sure it was leaking," says Thiêu. "We then emptied out the oil and used up all the fuel. That is how we did it, so our ship was no longer seaworthy."

An Interlude

But before Thiêu scuttled the boat, a serious matter arose that could have changed the course of the family's fortunes.

As mentioned, there were 17 Cao-Trúóng's on the boat and 10 members of a family that were close friends of Tô's father. They were a wealthy family who had managed to smuggle a large amount of gold onboard when they left Viêtnam.

During the first failed attempt to leave, the people responsible for taking both families from the shore to the boat had asked for 15 ounces of gold. The Cao-Trúóng's paid 7.5 ounces while the other family also paid 7.5 ounces. Even though the attempt failed, neither family was entitled to a refund.

"I was okay with that," says Thiêu. "In this type of business these things happen. It is the risk you take. They upheld their end of the bargain. It wasn't their fault that we got the day wrong."

Before the second, this time successful attempt at leaving, and in order to hurry things along, the Cao-Trúóng's had paid the family ferrying them to the boat the full 15 ounces of gold. The idea being, the other family would reimburse the Cao-Trúóng's their half share when they were at sea.

Fast-forward a few days later and they were sitting off the coast of Malaysia. Thiêu asked one of his relatives to take the family gold, and the 7.5 ounces they received from the other family, and make sure it was in a safe place. It was then that they realised nobody had collected the fee from the other family. No problem, thought Thiêu, I'll get them to pay now.

However, when Thiêu approached the patriarch, he refused to pay. He was in sight of land, safe from Viêtnamese authorities, and therefore, saw no reason why he had to pay.

Thiêu had already grown up in hardship and was no fool. He had endured much more than most before they started on this trip and was in no mood to play games.

In front of everyone, Thiêu made an announcement. He told his family to go to shore. The other family was going to stay onboard and Thiêu was going to take them back out to sea. The implication was that at least some of that family would not be coming back with him once he returned.

The patriarch's wife quickly resolved the issue by handing over the 7.5 ounces of gold. The crisis was averted, and everybody went onshore.

Chapter 12

Camp Life

Thiêu and the extended Cao-Trúóng clan arrived in Malaysia on October 17th, 1977.

"When we put all the people on the land, we had to wait on the beach for the UN authorities to come and list us and record our landing," says Thiêu. "The boards and planks from the boat helped make a temporary shelter against the elements."

From the time they had left the port in Việtnam, until they came under the protection of the UN, three days had passed. Once they got to the camp, they felt they had arrived in a safe, if somewhat crowded, haven.

The UN had living facilities, but the influx of people was too much, which meant the refugee camp was growing faster than the infrastructure.

"I felt safe in the camp," says Tô.

"Once they put down our names on the list, they gave us a site. Thiêu made a house for us with the planks. Then my

A Packet of Cigarettes

husband and the other men from the boat went into the forest and they got palm seed leaves and used them to cover the planks, which was our roof."

Tô knew there was going to be hard times ahead, but life was going to be okay. She didn't feel like her life was at risk anymore and she could move forward. She and Thiêu and the other adults took care of the children, plus the UN gave them staples to live on – like dry noodles and sardines.

"There was a lot of monotony, but we made do with what we had," she says. "There were rations they gave us every day. A little bit of beef and dried anchovies that we could rehydrate."

"The kids were fine. They just played," says Thiêu.

"They would wake up and hang around. Jennifer and Dianne took care of the smaller kids. Every few days or so, we would go into the local market. They would give us some money to buy food. The little bit of gold we had, we sold it, and we were able to buy fabric to make clothes and buy some extra food."

Although camp life was mundane, they quickly settled into a routine. Everybody pitched in. If you were a doctor in Viêtnam, then you put forward that skill to help the camp. If you were a carpenter or electrician, the same applied. Those who could speak English – or any other language – were in high demand. One thing that was apparent straight away was that being a refugee stripped all pretence of hierarchy.

"When you strip away all the wealth from others, the core of who you are is what you are," says Thiêu.

"You're not worried about who has more money, who has better things. It is survival mode – what food you have the next day. How do you get on with others? We were on a journey, so the next goal was to get to a new country."

Thiêu felt relief, but also apprehension. What would happen now? How long would they be in the camp? Who decided

Camp Life

where they would end up? Where did they want to go? Canada? Australia? The USA? Maybe New Zealand?

He had his preferences, but first he had to drink it all in. He felt he had secured a better future for his family, but what that future was had yet to be played out.

Thiêu knew where he didn't want to go – the USA. He still held animosity towards America's broken promises and the way it left South Viêtnam years earlier. That left choices between Australia, New Zealand and Canada. Canada was almost immediately ruled out of contention due to its proximity to the USA and its climate. That left Australia and New Zealand. With a bigger population and more opportunities, the consensus among the family was that Australia would be the best place for a new start.

"I was looking at my position, and the position of the countries that were available to us," says Thiêu. "I was hard working, and Australia was a big land with less people in it so there were more opportunities for me.

"I thought, if I fell on hard times, I can always go farming to support the family. My brother-in-law and I had discussed this before leaving Viêtnam, so we knew we were going to the same place. We never liked America as we felt America had let us down during the war and they abandoned us.

"There were options to go to Canada and New Zealand. The French navy would pick up boat people from the seas and take them to France. The French were out there before any other nation doing a lot of rescuing as they felt responsible, but we had no desire to go there. The Australian representative visited us early and the time for departure to go there was the quickest, so we chose that."

Not only did the Cao family choose the 'Lucky Country', but they also had another stroke of good fortune. Some of the people at the refugee camp had been there for the best part of

18 months. Yet, just after eight weeks, the Cao clan was off to Australia, arriving in Perth on Christmas Eve, 1977.

"Some refugees didn't bother going to other countries and wait to be processed, they went straight to Australia from Viêtnam," says Thiêu.

"They landed by boat in Darwin, which prompted the Australian government to process people early, because if not, the influx of refugees would go straight to Australia, similar to what started happening later in the 2000s.

"They wanted more control so word got out that the Australian government would process arrivals in Asian refugee camps quickly. We happened to arrive at the time the Australian government decided to be more proactive."

Of the 27 people on the boat, 26 went to Perth while one chose to live in New Zealand.

A Packet of Cigarettes

Thi Tô at 16 years of age.

Portrait of Thiêu as a young man.

A Packet of Cigarettes

A 24-year-old Thiêu at Soc Trang.

Tô and Thiêu on their wedding day – August 8, 1966.

A Packet of Cigarettes

The Cao family shortly before their departure from Viêtnam. From left – Joanne, Tô, Chris, Thiêu, Dianne, Jennifer.

Newly arrived refugees at the Pulau Besar Refugee Camp, Malasyia. Note that the hut behind them was recycled from the parts of the boat that was purposely wrecked when the family arrived in Malaysia.

A Packet of Cigarettes

Thiêu and Joanne at the refugee camp in Malaysia. Thieu copying music tapes from one cassette tape to another.

Thiêu posing on steps in Malaysia.

A Packet of Cigarettes

The Cao family making their way from the refugee camp to the airport in Kuala Lumpur. Tô (in yellow) holding Jo and helping Chris. Dianne being helped on shore by man in yellow (far right).

Getting off the boat to go to the airport. Tô in yellow being helped off with Chris and Joanne. Jennifer (in red) looks on.

A Packet of Cigarettes

Thiêu and Chris on the aeroplane taking them to Perth. Tô is next to Thieu.

Kids' first family portrait in King's Park, Perth. Clockwise from bottom – Joanne, Chris, Jennifer, Dianne.

A Packet of Cigarettes

Tô and Thiêu in their lounge in Flemington, Sydney circa 1981. Note the portrait of Tô's father on the mantlepiece.

Cao family at a family wedding held at Auburn's Botanical Gardens in Sydney. From left – Jennifer, Chris, Dianne, Tô, Thiêu and Joanne.

A Packet of Cigarettes

First family wedding in Sydney circa 1980/81.

Tô and Thiêu at their new home in Penrith, circa 1985/6.

A Packet of Cigarettes

Thiêu and Tô's 30th wedding anniversary. From left: Joanne, Thieu, Jennifer, Chris, Dianne; seated Tô.

A Packet of Cigarettes

Tô and Thiêu partaking in one of their favourite pastimes – ballroom dancing.

Tô and Thiêu ballroom dancing.

A Packet of Cigarettes

Thiêu and Tô at their 50th wedding anniversary with Dianne as MC.

Grandchildren – from left Anabelle and Teagan (Dianne's daughters); Martine, Caitlin and Liam (Joanne's children); Kenneth (Dianne's son); Sarah and Stephanie (Jennifer's daughters); and Loan (Kenneth's wife).

A Packet of Cigarettes

Thiêu and Tô (sitting on couch at right) with their children, grandchildren and extended family.

Chapter 13

A New Home

FORTUNE IS SOMETHING THAT HAD BEEN LACKING in the Cao household in terms of material wealth. Viêtnam was a third-world country and by the time the Communists took over, nothing much had changed, and it wasn't about to.

One of the mantras of Communism is that everybody is created equal and therefore the wealth should be distributed accordingly – everybody gets their fair share. This did occur – as long as you were a Communist Party member. Thiêu knew this, which is why when he and his family hopped on a plane heading for Perth, he felt like the luckiest man in the world.

Some would call it luck, others good planning. Whichever way you looked at it, the Cao's were on their way to a new life.

In the early 1970s, Australia had rejected its White Australia Policy with the Gough Whitlam government in 1975, making it illegal to reject an immigration application based on race. When Whitlam was sacked as Prime Minister in 1975, the

A Packet of Cigarettes

incoming Liberal Government led by Malcolm Fraser embraced the idea of skilled immigrants coming from different parts of the world to make up the shortfall in labour. It was also a time when unskilled workers in the form of refugees from conflicts in Southeast Asia would be heading towards Australian borders.

Like the skilled labour, Fraser welcomed the influx of refugees. While his initial acceptance was based on humanitarian reasons, decades later, the success of his decision can be seen in the many small businesses and multi-cultural contributions the people from Southeast Asia have given to the country.

Thiêu never forgot the moment they arrived in Australia.

"It was early in the morning when we arrived in Perth," he says. "I realised how beautiful it was when we saw the lights.

"I found flying very strange. You board and then you wonder what is going on. I was anxious mainly due to the novelty of it. You don't know what is going to happen next. As soon as we landed, we knew we were in a developed country. The landscape was different. It was a different world. I was thinking 'How do you walk into this world and survive in it?' It is what we had to do."

Not wanting to waste any time, the family was keen to start work straight away. Thiêu said their goal was to be independent and not rely on others.

"Hard work wasn't the problem," he says. "We needed work as we had four kids. I had to feed them. The hardest part was trying to understand English.

"We had to go the unskilled labour route. Even the average unskilled person in Australia at the time didn't want to do the hard manual labour-type jobs. If they were literate, they didn't want to do that for a living."

The family started living in a hostel and learning English was a priority. Upon arrival in Australia, they were entitled

A New Home

to Centrelink money, with the hostel taking 60-70 percent of the funds to go toward housing and utility costs. The Cao's were left with about 30 percent of that money for themselves, but Thiêu didn't like relying on handouts. The family stayed at the hostel for three months before they ended up finding a place of their own.

When it came to arriving in Australia, it was about survival. To them – it was just base level survival – nothing that they hadn't already gone through in Viêtnam.

"Over there, you had a cottage with a leaf roof and now there is a brick house in Australia," says Thiêu.

"This was completely new to us. It was hard and then you take another step, and it got harder, but we met every hurdle. We knew we had made the right decision, and we were excited, but we also knew the way ahead was going to be hard. Getting work wasn't going to be easy.

"For us, the issue was trying to find out about everything new. Trying to get used to how things were done here. The economic climate, which was not great at time, was not on our radar. We were learning how to survive. We just needed food, shelter, and clothing – all the important things. We didn't even know what vacuuming was when we first came over."

Years later, he still knows it's the best decision he ever made.

"We don't regret coming here at all," says Thiêu.

Chapter 14

The Locals

O NCE THE 'WHITES-ONLY AUSTRALIA' POLICY had been abandoned, and Australia met its obligation in taking in refugees, the cultural landscape of the country began to change. Refugees from both the Viêtnam War and Lebanon Civil War started arriving in the country. To meet skills shortages, others started arriving too from the Balkans, Southern Europe and traditional migrant starting points such as the UK and New Zealand.

The Cao's had to learn quickly to adapt. Thiêu didn't feel there was any blatant racism towards the family. He felt there were other issues at play.

"I didn't think about it," he says. "There were differences, and I could tell that some of them were trying to make me feel uncomfortable.

"But I think it was more that they had a different way of doing things. In Australia, Western people talk to each other in a quieter tone, but we are used to speaking loudly and

The Locals

abrasive and therefore, we come across different. I was too busy trying to keep up than try to justify my position to anyone. I was concentrating on how to blend into my surroundings and make sure I didn't make mistakes at work."

As for the other members of the family, they saw some racism. They knew it was out there but didn't talk about it. They were more concerned about making a living, how to make money and raise their children.

"Prejudice or racism happens in every country," says Thiêu. "Even in China and Viêtnam, people are prejudice against other people. They are more subtle in Asia.

"In some cultures, it is blatant and in your face. I found the amount of racism in Australia very small compared to Viêtnam and other countries I have visited since leaving. Chinese people are the worst when it comes to racism. The Chinese people who live in Viêtnam are very racist towards the Viêtnamese and I'm saying that as a Chinese-Viêtnamese person. They don't marry the Viêtnamese because they think they are better."

Thiêu found Australian people gentler and kinder compared to some cultures.

"In some places you go, if you speak the language, they'll be selling something for $1, but as soon as they see a foreigner, they'll sell it to you for $10," he says.

Thiêu said when they arrived it didn't take them long to realise how well Australia took care of its elderly and its young. While some Australians may disagree, Thiêu would invite them to go live in Viêtnam or other third-world country and compare. He likes the security Australia has to offer.

"Everyone gets a place to live, and everybody gets the opportunity to work and contribute," he says.

Chapter 15

Working

Initially, there was little work available for the Viêtnamese in Australia. Tô was the first member of the family to get a job. She worked at the Western Ocean Fish Canning factory. The family had arrived in Perth at the right time. While there was high inflation, there was plenty of work because the locals thought factory work was below them, so it was ripe for job-hungry refugees and migrants.

"A lot of young white people didn't want to do that type of work. It was a dirty job," says Tô.

"The factory nearly went broke because they couldn't get workers. The ones that were there were lazy and just waiting for a paycheck every week instead of working. Productivity was very low. The company was losing money."

This is when Tô thinks luck intervened for the Cao's. The company hired a Korean man who asked the cannery's owners to subcontract the workforce to him and he would manage the labour. The Korean and his workforce produced the canned

Working

goods and were paid by the owners on what was produced. He initially hired a lot of Korean people but there wasn't enough of them. He was married to a Viêtnamese woman, which is how they initially got a couple of Viêtnamese boat people to work in the factory.

"His wife got in a few and they did really well," says Thiêu.

"My wife knew the lady and she applied and got a job. There were refugee immigrants dying to get these jobs and they worked hard to get things done. The owners could see that the new employees were hard workers. When the contract ended with the Korean man, the owners took over the hiring themselves."

With four young mouths to feed, Thiêu and Tô got stuck into work, with Thiêu soon working the night shift at the factory. He was used as a translator even though his English was poor.

"I didn't know too much English, but I knew their body language and they understood mine," he says.

However, the pay wasn't that great. They calculated that once they factored in taxes, Tô was $7 worse off a week than being on the country's social security system.

"But I said to her that she had to work so we could be self-sufficient," says Thiêu. "If the two of us work, we could get ahead. But if it was just one of us working, then it wasn't worth it. That is how we saved and got ahead."

The work was hard, but it wasn't as laborious compared to what Thiêu did as a boy in Viêtnam. Shift work was one challenge. Understanding how the various machines worked was another, as well as getting used to the day-to-day life of living in a new country.

In Viêtnam, there was no such thing as a weekend. They worked every day to survive. They needed to get to the know the lay of the land better. They ended up staying in Perth for just over two years.

A Packet of Cigarettes

The family had always been ambitious, and while Perth offered them a lot, the Eastern Seaboard offered more opportunities. They made the decision to move to Sydney in late 1979. The key motivation was that Tô's mother had arrived in the country and had decided to stay with one of her other children based in Sydney.

When the Cao's first settled in Australia, the law stated that they had to stay in the same city where the immigration department settled them. By the time Tô's mother arrived, there was a family reunion policy that allowed families to move to cities where other relatives lived.

Chapter 16

Sydney

WHEN THEY MOVED FROM PERTH, they first set up in Burwood, which was then considered part of the Sydney's outer West. Four decades later, it would become part of the inner West as Sydney quadrupled in size. They would later move out a couple of suburbs to Lidcombe.

"We found that life in Sydney was a bit easier, and it was more cosmopolitan," says Thiêu.

"Perth was very white. There were not many Viêtnamese in Perth. In Sydney, you could go to Chinatown and there were similar skinned people there.

"There were a lot of Hong Kong and Singapore immigrants, and you could go and ask them for jobs, and they wouldn't shun you. A lot of Viêtnamese can speak Chinese. And we could understand them better than English. About 70 to 80 percent of Viêtnamese can speak a Chinese language."

In Asia, there is a pecking order when it comes to cultures. Thiêu knew this and while that order has changed over the years, when they arrived in Sydney, he knew who ruled the roost.

"The Chinese people believe they are at the top of the pile," he says.

"Back in the day, in the 1980s, Hong Kong was the leading Westernised Asian culture. They felt they were better than other Asian cultures. If you want to be in their world, you had to speak their language. Today, Korea is the pop culture that Asian kids are attracted to."

It helped that the Cao family were Teo Cheow, which meant they understood some Cantonese. Thiêu considers himself Viêtnamese, despite his Chinese ancestry.

"I am more Viêtnamese than Chinese," he says. "When I lie awake at night, I think in terms of being Viêtnamese. I know everything about Viêtnam. I can speak a Chinese language, and I try to understand my roots in China, but I don't think like a Chinese person."

Another reason for moving to Sydney was the number of job opportunities. Thiêu's brother-in-law found him a position in a restaurant washing dishes. The pay was relatively modest, with Thiêu bringing home $280 a week, almost $100 more than factory jobs were paying at the time.

"It was a dirty job – washing all the time," he says. "A lot of smells. A lot of people did not like working there. We wanted the money. You need a lot of money, and we didn't have anything then. You had to survive in a new country. It was not an open society to us. Our opportunities were narrow."

Thiêu had developed a good work ethic since childhood. It is something that he has instilled in his four children. His penchant for working hard soon caught the eye of the restaurant owner.

"Every morning, I came in early to start my shift. I was always the first one there," he says.

Sydney

"I had to clean the kitchen and prepare for the chef. Soon, they tapped my shoulder as they were opening a new restaurant, and they wanted me to work there. They guaranteed me $400 a week. No-one worked as hard as me because I was hungry to make money. I worked six days a week and had one day off – not over the weekend because we were busy."

Immigrants like Thiêu were ripe to be exploited by others. He ended up leaving the job at the restaurant after an incident with the restaurant owner's daughter. One day, he turned up for his shift and was ushered into the owner's office. The daughter had lost her watch. She had left it on a side table in an office at the restaurant and it went missing. She blamed Thiêu and he was furious.

Straight away, he went and got his work bag and emptied it out in front of the boss. Nothing was there. He then went to the rear of the premises and emptied the rubbish bins. Again, nothing there. While Thiêu was subservient to his boss, after a couple of hours, he decided to draw a line in the sand. He told his boss that if they hadn't found the watch within 24 hours, he would leave the job. As it turned out, the daughter found it at home. She had forgotten to put it on. Although Thiêu kept his promise and returned to work, he left soon after.

"I left one week later and soon had another job in a plastic recycling plant," he says. "Not long after, I ran into the restaurant owner's son, and he asked me to come back. He wanted to pay me more money, but I couldn't go back out of pride."

After several years of working hard, Thiêu and Tô had enough money for a deposit on a house. While Cabramatta was the hub of the Viêtnamese community in Sydney, it was also home to some unsavoury aspects. This was the late 1980s. While coming to a new country had brought a lot of benefits to immigrants, many traumatised migrants turned to drugs, especially heroin. While Thiêu and Tô's children were well disciplined, the parents didn't want any distractions that would have an adverse effect on their lives during their formative years.

"One day, we went shopping in Cabramatta and Bonnyrigg, just feeling out the environment," says Thiêu.

"I decided it wasn't a good place because there were many Viêtnamese kids that were not being attended to. Parents were working all day, and the kids were left alone. There seemed to be a lot of street kids. I didn't think Cabramatta would be good for the children especially if my wife and I had to work long hours and were not around. They would be influenced by other Viêtnamese kids."

With that in mind, they bought a house in the far west of Sydney, in Penrith, at the foot of the Blue Mountains.

Chapter 17

Penrith

The move to Penrith in Sydney's far west came as a culture shock to Thiêu's two eldest children, Jennifer and Dianne. Both were in their teens when they moved out west, and both were out of their comfort zone as few Asian families lived there.

Thiêu knew that the state government was keen to push the expanding city westward, which meant housing was more affordable. The house they bought cost just shy of $50,000, while houses in other parts of the city, where extended family members lived, cost almost $80,000.

"I was looking at a reasonable house at an affordable price in a decent area. I thought it was a good place for children," he says.

"When I made the decision to move, I accepted the consequences of what was going to happen. I was isolating my children from their community. I knew I was distancing myself from the rest of the family, but that wasn't my goal. My goal was protecting the children from other parts. For me, that was a price I was willing to take to make sure my kids didn't go astray."

Dianne remembers being racially abused by classmates. While she was strong enough to look after herself, years later, she wondered whether it was a good idea for them to move there. Both of her parents were seldom around.

Thiêu had to leave very early in the morning and came home late at night as he was working in North Sydney and the Northern Beaches, 90 minutes away in traffic. He had qualified as a carpenter and worked on renovation projects. Tô stayed with relatives in the inner west during the week as she had a factory job nearby and would only join the family on weekends. This meant that Jennifer and Dianne had to juggle their school workload and look after their two younger siblings.

Thirty years later, Thiêu defends his decision. The housing was affordable, and it allowed him to raise his children in what he considered a safer environment from where they had come. And it allowed them to immerse themselves in the new culture.

"Socially, family is everything. I preferred to be with family," he says. "I have never had a strong opinion of friends. I don't trust them as much; therefore, I don't have a lot of friends. My extended family was my social group, and I operated within that.

"I realised that my kids needed to become part of the Western culture. As hard as it is for me to speak English now, it would be just as hard for them to speak Viêtnamese. I understood that it was going to happen. I had to embrace the change. If you move to a new country, you must change. You can't expect not to.

"I am a progressive thinker. I might not have much education but being the man of the family, you must think ahead. If you make a wrong decision, your family might go downhill.

Penrith

"I avoided the massive drug problem in Cabramatta in the 80s. I thought my kids might be persuaded to do bad things. I thought that if I keep them out of there, when they are older, they will make better decisions."

Thiêu was concerned how his two older daughters would adapt. He might not have been educated, but he knew that both of his daughters would attract the attention of prospective paramours, and he wasn't wrong. As they entered their mid-teens, both girls attracted a lot of attention. But both were also aware of Asian norms when it came to sex. It was a no-no.

"I was concerned about the girls because they were attractive, and boys might come along and cavort with them," says Thiêu.

"They might not have been street smart enough to know any different. As for being in both worlds, that is a hard question. Every society has good and bad things about it. And there are different good and bad things within different cultures."

Thiêu realised, over the years, the many European Australians resent cultures that do not try to assimilate, especially those from a non-European background. Thiêu agrees that assimilation is important. However, migrants who have been established in the country for generations need to be patient. He also believes immigrants need to respect the country they arrive in and the cultures that are already established.

"If you think your way is better and the other way is no good when you arrive, then you already have a superiority complex," he says.

"But if you ask yourself 'Why is he doing that?' then you find out they do it for a reason. People have to understand that most people who come to Australia are doing so to better their lives, not disrupt other's lives. Some of the things we do are for safety and security. After that, we can go out and assimilate. It is gradual though. It will not happen overnight."

A Packet of Cigarettes

He believes it takes a generation to change.

"For example, my generation speaks very loudly, and I can see that the next generation is different," he says. "It is hard to change things."

While Thiêu believed his decision was sound, Dianne still isn't sold on the idea when they moved suburbs. One of her main objections was more to do with the socio-economic landscape than culture. Like a lot of the Western suburbs in Sydney, Penrith was working class to the bone. This meant a lot of the inhabitants were not academic and were more likely to take up an apprenticeship or a TAFE course over university.

Dianne's ambition was to go to university. She was an able student, hard worker and did well in her exams. She was keen to work in the medical field – dentistry, pharmacy, or even medicine. Unfortunately, with the way the Australian secondary school system worked in terms of external exam results, her dreams might have been shattered before she even sat her final exams.

"I told Mum and Dad to leave Penrith because all the kids around us were disinterested in tertiary education," she says.

"I did okay, but once I went through the HSC, I understood the scaling of HSC marks, and what school you go to affects your university entrance score. Because a lot of my peers were not academic, they pulled down the marks of the whole cohort."

Thiêu reasoned with Tô that, later in life, the kids would thank him and be mature enough to understand why he did what he did when moving out west. He never saw Penrith as a permanent place of residency and knew that one day they would be moving back to be near the extended family.

"I made sure my kids got to the next level in their lives instead of being dragged down," he says.

"Even today, I can't anything good about Cabramatta. The good parts get around a 3/10. The bad parts around

Penrith

5/10. The good bits are small, and the bad bits are bigger than the good."

Thiêu did recognise it was important that his children get a good education. What they did after that was up to them.

"I wanted all the kids to get a degree," he says.

"I had no aspirations of where they should go. I just wanted them to make a good living and be educated. The Viêtnamese community value an educated person. When you are educated, you see and rationalise things differently. I didn't want them to be ignorant. As a generation, I wanted to sacrifice my life for them. I wanted them to step on my shoulders and go further. Then when my kids become parents, they can pave the way for their children, so they can step on their shoulders and so on."

Thiêu remembers what education would have been like under the Communist Viêtnamese government. Years one through to five were free. After that, it was user pays. And being a Communist country, those that belonged to the 'Party' got preference, which meant most Viêtnamese went without further education.

Both Dianne and Joanne ended up getting pharmacy degrees, while Jennifer ended up getting married and moving to Perth before coming back to Sydney. Chris got 9/10ths of the way through a Land Economics degree before his career took him in a different direction. Overall, all the children did well for themselves – Thiêu and Tô are confident they made the right decision to leave Viêtnam, as well as move to Penrith.

The family ended up living in Penrith for five years. As if to prove Dianne's point that it wasn't a great idea, when they arrived at their brand-new house, somebody had ripped out their new hot-water system, so there was no hot water. The builders took advantage of the naivety of the family saying that since the contract had been signed, it wasn't the builder's problem. It would take almost 18 months before the family would get a replacement system.

In the end, Dianne convinced her father to leave.

"I told Dad that if he let Chris and Joanne do their HSC there, their university prospects would be diminished," she says.

"He moved them out straight away. Chris went to another school – Homebush Boys. At least there were kids there who were driven, and the school had better resources. If you are at a poor school, they allocate resources to truancy, kids misbehaving and smoking and all that stuff. No one is dealing with somebody getting good grades. Mum and Dad wanted good results."

Chapter 18

Back in the Fold

Despite Thiêu not being a fan of Cabramatta, he moved the family back there to be nearer to the Viêtnamese community. He also started a photography business. That didn't mean he was happy being there. His reasons for returning were more to do with the practicality of his work.

"I moved back to Cabramatta because it was close to work, and things had changed. My business partner was my nephew, and he had kids there," says Thiêu.

"We also thought the kids were old enough to understand what was right and wrong. Sometime later, when I sold the business, I didn't want to live there anymore so we moved to Lidcombe."

Thiêu's move was not only because he thought it was a better area in terms of house prices.

"I don't identify completely with the Viêtnamese community and culture in Australia in general," he says.

A Packet of Cigarettes

"What I can say about the Viêtnamese community is that it tends not to assimilate, and people stay in their own ways. They don't take on new ways of thinking or doing, and therefore they don't learn, which means a certain generation stay uneducated and ignorant. I was always open-minded and progressive and looking at new ways of doing things."

Dianne agrees with her father. Having been around the community, Dianne believes her father is a maverick in terms of how he sees the world. A lot of Viêtnamese men bring their friends home, show them a lot of respect, make a banquet, and the wives prepare food, make sure there is alcohol, and make sure the friends are being taken care of.

Thiêu never did any of that. He rarely drank, which could have been a result of his mother's alcohol-related death.

"It is something that a lot of Viêtnamese women do by looking after their husbands," says Dianne. "It's a celebration but the men do it every weekend and they value their male peer company immensely.

"They spend a lot of their attention on that. They make their wives spend a lot of time cooking. As women, we labour over the meals and serve up these delights. Although I never had this experience it in my family, I saw many women put a meal on the table and then move to separate quarters. I find the patriarchy hard to digest and although it is part of my culture, I did not like it. I thought, 'I'm not going anywhere near that'.

"My family never had any of these nights. Luckily, my ex-husband Tony, like my father, was not keen on these types of events and so we had very minimal 'drinking' gatherings."

Looking back on his life, Thiêu knows that by Viêtnamese standards – Asian morals in general – his life had not been run of the mill. He was initially not accepted into the community and was seen as a little wild.

Back in the Fold

He remembered a lot of people giving him side glances and whispering behind his back. More than once he heard them calling him a 'bad kid' because they would judge him and thought he lacked structure growing up as an orphan. That is why he was grateful his aunt Thi Lang took him under her wing after the death of his parents. All those experiences led him to be the man he was and raise the family the way he did.

Both Dianne and Jennifer believe they have long-lasting trauma from their past, but they are also thankful their parents took them from Viêtnam. Having visited it several times since they left, they know that they would have had a much harder life if they had stayed.

Thiêu, too, has learned a lot. By the time he married, he knew that the most important thing in his life would be his family and since the children were born, that has been the case.

Chapter 19

Family

"**B**Y THE TIME I GOT MARRIED, I realised I had to be more family focused," Thiêu says.

"When I became a father, I evolved a lot. I understood that you couldn't say to children 'Do as I say not as I do.'. You've got to change yourself. For example, if I don't want my kids to watch TV, I've got learn to not watch TV. I understood that I had to model the right behaviour. If you expect kids not to do something, you have to learn not to do it yourself."

What Thiêu didn't miss were some of the old traditions. He abandoned tradition to make way for science and modern technology. One of the things he happily embraced when he arrived on Australian shores was how the country was set up to be run on practical outcomes not tradition and superstition. He cited the example of the Viêtnamese tradition of giving women more salt after giving birth.

"Women became swollen up because of water retention," he says.

Family

"Water wasn't going out. It was terrible. They had to subject themselves to that in the name of tradition. It was their way of recovering from childbirth. There was no science behind it."

Viêtnam puts a lot of stock in having a big family. This is because it helps everyone carry the load. The more children you have, the more they can look after you when you are older and the more than can contribute to the family. It was not unusual for couples to have seven or eight children. While Thiêu was one of four kids, Tô was one of eight. When it came to Thiêu and Tô having their own children, they stopped at four.

"I stopped at four because that was the right number for me. The Communists also said you were not allowed to have too many kids. You couldn't afford it. You have to be happy with what you have. You can't be unhappy with what you don't have. I congratulated my wife on having so many daughters because now the house would always be clean," he laughed. "I looked for the practical side."

Chapter 20

Cultural Values

ONE OF THE MAIN ISSUES when coming to a foreign country is the difference in cultural values. Emigrating from one Asian country to another can have its own pitfalls. However, when emigrating to a foreign continent that you have nothing in common with culturally – whether as a refugee or through normal channels – there are a plethora of other challenges. Most Asian cultures are similarly aligned in their value systems, but there are other barriers such as food, language and politics. Coming to a Western country exacerbates the adaptation process.

Thiêu knew it wasn't going to be an easy integration process. It was an interesting proposition because, unlike a lot of first-generation immigrants, Thiêu embraced the cultural differences of Australia. He felt that the country's culture prepared him much better to be part of a society.

"Instead of teaching you how to pay respect to your elders and say 'yes', the Western culture teaches you that at 18, you have the right to be an adult," he says.

Cultural Values

"You have to go into society, you have to make a living, and you have to get a position there. You make your mark in society. Whereas with Asian culture, you make your mark in the family.

"When you teach the Viêtnamese way, it fits into your family, but it doesn't allow you to integrate into society as much. Each family will have different values. The Viêtnamese culture teaches you things that will suit the Viêtnamese country. Within your ethnicity, you will be able to function well, but outside of your own ethnicity, things don't mix as well."

As mentioned, Thiêu was a bit of an anomaly in his culture after being pushed to independence at a young age. Like both of his older children, he recognised that self-development was an important part of 'making it' in the world, whether that be Australia or Viêtnam.

As with most cultures, saving or giving face, is when you don't try and embarrass, or put under the microscope, the flaws of those around you. While not a trait that can solely be said to be part of Asian cultures, in some cases, it is implemented to the nth degree. It's something that Thiêu was never a fan of, even growing up.

"As an Asian man in the Viêtnamese culture, I can only be progressive so much," he says.

"I can't change fully. What I don't like about saving face is the inability to identify your own flaws and then fix them. You have to have the courage to face your own flaws. People save face to look good, but the problem with doing that is you do it so much that you don't even know what your defects are. And if you don't know what your defects are, you won't be able to fix them."

Caught between two worlds, Thiêu and Tô had very few close friends in their forties and fifties. Those closest to them

A Packet of Cigarettes

were their four children, and Tô's brothers and sisters who made the journey to Australia. They were happy in their own company and that of their family. However, in retirement their social group grew, and they now belong to many vibrant groups with interests such as ballroom dancing, travelling and ping pong events. Thiêu has taken up learning the keyboard whereby he plays the instrument at church and the Lidcombe social group based in Sydney's inner west.

Would they have more friends if they had stayed in Viêtnam? Most likely. But one of the costs of coming to a country that was so culturally different from their own was always going to be that they would have to make sacrifices to give their children a better life.

"I did have some friends, but I was picky about who they were," Thiêu says.

"I don't welcome just anybody into my house. I had young impressionable daughters at home, and I didn't want drunk men taking advantage of them. A drunk bunch of 10 men – some will behave appropriately, but some might not, and how do you protect against that?"

Thiêu is philosophical about his expectations coming to Australia. As a European-based culture, he knew before he landed on Australian shores that there would be different values his children and grandchildren would take onboard. It was probably harder for his kids, because they grew up in two worlds, whereas his grandchildren would have the benefit of Asian-Asian or Asian-European parents who had grown up in a Eurocentric country. They would be fluent in English but not Viêtnamese.

As it turned out, his two younger children barely speak Viêtnamese, while his two eldest children speak what Dianne considers to be pidgin Viêtnamese. As for his eight grandchildren, three can slightly understand the language and

Cultural Values

are learning to speak it, while the remaining five can neither speak nor understand it.

"I would like them to retain some culture, but you can't enforce it, and you can't make them do it," he says. "In that respect, I learned to expect that parts of our Việtnamese culture will fade.

"It's like the shrine on the mantlepiece to our parents that all Việtnamese migrants of my generation have. I'm guessing that by my grandkid's generation, it will be gone."

Chapter 21

The Kids

When their son Chris was 18, he decided to tell his parents that he was gay. Thiêu and Tô arranged a dinner with a young girl who had shown some interest in him. Both sets of parents turned up but neither of the children did. It was then that Chris came out to his parents. At the time, Thiêu was so angry he lashed out.

"I blamed my wife," he says. "The reason I blamed my wife was that she told me to give him his independence. I was trying to stop him doing things and be a dutiful son. I blamed her, but she didn't fight back. I feel bad about that now because she didn't want him to be gay any more than I wanted him to be, but she bore the brunt of my wrath."

"I was sad, and I cried, and I was shocked," says Tô. "He was 18, which is young. I didn't know what to do. He was delivering pizza and working late hours, and we attributed that to the lifestyle he was living. I spoke to my older brother, who was

The Kids

closely linked to the Catholic church. I thought we might go and talk to the priest."

Thiêu and Tô are now accepting of Chris's sexuality. Upon reflection, Thiêu believes his elder brother could have been gay. He never had a girlfriend and was very good looking. However, being openly gay in 1950s and 1960s Việtnam was not an option. Both parents now only want Chris to be happy.

"We are okay with it now," says Thiêu. "He didn't choose to be gay. As parents, we need to support him. He lives a happy life, so we don't base our happiness on where he is. Our happiness is dependent on ourselves.

"I don't believe that being gay is a choice. I think that is the way some people are. There was a disappointment at the beginning because he was my only son, and I wanted him to carry on my name. It bothered me but I had to make peace with it. There are no more Cao's after us. My brother died, so Chris and I were the only ones with the name. That made me upset. If my brother had a boy or I had more, it would have been different. We hid it from the family for a while. We didn't really know how to deal with it."

Only in the past Ten yearshave they been able to accept it. Thiêu said from the 1980s to the early 2000s they had to get it right for themselves first, so they rarely talked about it. They skirted around the topic, even when people made comments such as "Oh, you have a son that isn't married," and they would say he just doesn't want to get married.

Middle daughter Dianne remembers one incident where an elaborate guise had to be implemented when her parents celebrated one of their milestone wedding anniversaries.

"Chris wanted to invite his partner Paul to the dinner. For Paul to be invited, Chris had to organise a table of male and female friends so Paul could be there under the guise of being a friend. He wasn't out as Chris's partner; he was just part of the group. That was about 12 years ago. The past seven years it has mellowed. Up until that point, it was very hard."

In the late 1980s, the eldest daughter Jennifer got married. While the Viêtnamese do not strictly arrange marriages, parents do try and tee up possible suiters. Generally, it is the grooms' parents who do the arranging, but it can vary. In the case of Jennifer, her husband-to-be, Van, was the son of an acquaintance of Tô's. It was someone she had met in Perth.

Getting married is a serious business in Asian culture. Thiêu and Tô's marriage ended up being something they both wanted, but not her parents. In most cases, both sets of parents want to know what the background the bride or groom come from, their employment prospects and how they hold themselves in the community.

In Jennifer's case, according to Tô, the groom's parents pushed the union. She seems to think it might have been a scheme by his mother because Jennifer's soon-to-be husband already had a girlfriend in Perth, but his mother didn't like her. They were in love, but his mother decided to find a prospective bride for him.

"I think they came over with an agenda already, because when they did come over, they were bearing gifts," says Tô.

"The boy and his father came over to Sydney to visit relatives and they came and visited us, and they saw Jennifer. After they went back to Perth, his mother called me, and we started a conversation about them getting together."

"When they asked about Jennifer, my wife spoke to the elders within the family as to whether it was a good idea or not," says Thiêu.

"Then we had to ask Jennifer if she wanted to go ahead with it. With most arranged marriages both people have to be happy with it. Back in the old days, it might be different, but we are a modern family. We still need elders to make the introduction, but the people have to agree to it.

The Kids

"At the time, we had limited knowledge about the family. All we were looking at was the fact they seemed like decent people, they were hard working, and they wanted to go into business. That fact they wanted to do business means they had a way of making a living. At least we knew that they could provide for our daughter and offspring.

"If I had looked a little deeper, I might have thought twice about Jennifer marrying into the family for a variety of reasons. You think differently back then. You have three daughters, and you have to marry them off somewhere."

Thiêu thought he was doing the right thing by Jennifer, but it didn't work out. Jennifer ended up moving to Perth and became involved in the family business, but not in a meaningful way.

Within five years, she was back in Sydney and Van followed her. However, the marriage only lasted a while longer and he went back to Perth. Since that time, both her daughters, Stephanie and Sarah, have remained estranged from their father who remarried and had more children. Stephanie married Hamish McIntosh in 2023.

Both Tô and Thiêu were upset at Jennifer's failed marriage. At the time, there were a lot of recriminations throughout the family. However, as time has gone by, both parents now see things differently.

"Looking back, I feel like Jennifer didn't have too much to do with the situation," says Thiêu. "I felt the problem lay with the mother-in-law because she was the matriarch of the family, and she was the puppeteer of the whole family.

"One time I went over to Perth when Dianne was opening her pharmacy, and the mother said to me 'don't worry about Jennifer. I am taking very good care of her. I'm always on her side and protecting her. It doesn't matter what happens I always tell my family that they are wrong, and Jennifer is always right'."

A Packet of Cigarettes

Thiêu knows that the mother was trying to reassure him, but it ended up having the opposite effect. He knew that elevating and putting Jennifer on a pedestal would not be doing her any favours when it came to the dynamics of the family – especially when it came to her sisters-in-law who were already established in the family.

"I said to her, 'By doing that, what you are doing is creating a schism in the family because you have Jennifer and husband on your side and the rest of the siblings on the other side,'" says Thiêu.

"'You can't do that; you have to be fair. When you are not fair in your decisions, you are setting them all against Jennifer and her husband'.

"What she was doing was elevating my daughter and her son to the status of being better than the others. Jennifer will have her own story on how it happened, but that is all I know. From the mother-in-law's perspective, she is trying to save face as well."

Being brought up in an Asian household in a Western country meant that the Cao siblings knew that things were different in Australia. Asian communities generally have a 'we' mindset as opposed to a 'me' one. Straddling between the two cultures was a bridge too far for Jennifer during her marriage, especially when she was part of a family that wasn't hers by blood.

"Jennifer didn't know what she was getting into," says Dianne. "She was young. For example, the bride's jewellery is hers. It belongs to the bride. She received it from all members of her family and her husband's and Jennifer should have been the one to have it for safe keeping. Her mother-in-law took all the jewellery and put it away in the safe. Then the money that they all made from the Asian grocery business; Jennifer didn't get a wage. Everyone would put money towards a house,

The Kids

but it was never a house for her and her husband. It was like wage theft. There was no spare money for individuals. Then the mother-in-law would add all the money together and buy a house or property for one of Jennifer's husband's siblings."

As luck would have it, Dianne's sister-in-law, Trúóng Hong Phuong (who was not only Dianne's husband's sister, but also married to a first cousin of the Cao siblings, which was how Dianne met her husband) managed to get the jewellery back for her.

On a trip to Perth, Jennifer confided to Phuong how unhappy she was and the reasons why, and also that she had no means to support herself due to the communal style of living. Seeing the issue, the sister-in-law asked her if she was so unhappy, why not use the jewellery as collateral, or cash some of it in, and head back to Sydney. That is when Jennifer told her about the mother-in-law having it in a safe, giving Jennifer no access.

Seeing the situation for what it was, Phuong decided to take matters into her own hands. On the pretence of not knowing which piece of jewellery she had given Jennifer for her wedding; she asked the mother-in-law if she could be reminded what it looked like. Once all the jewellery was laid out in front of her, and after an appropriate time of admiring it, and then pointing out the piece she had given Jennifer, she bundled up the whole collection and handed it to Jennifer, saying – in a nice way – "This is yours, you should be the one to keep it safe and not burden you mother-in-law with looking after it."

Thiêu's second daughter, Dianne, had an ambition to make something of herself – no matter the cost. Having arrived in Australia when she was seven, she remembers little of Viêtnam. She only knows that being the type of personality she is – feisty, non-conforming, and an extreme dislike for the

A Packet of Cigarettes

patriarchal tenets of Asian culture – she would have caused a heap of trouble for her family if they had stayed in Viêtnam.

Growing up, she was compliant with her parent's wishes, but she sees now – in retrospect – that as she grew older, doing something because 'it's just the way things are' would not have followed her into adulthood.

As a teenager, going to school in Penrith as one of only three Asian kids (one of the others being her sister Jennifer), she embraced Western culture.

"The environment in Viêtnam when I was born wasn't a good one," says Dianne. "They had a curfew, and I was born in a barn. I think that led to some of the health problems I have now such as asthma. There was one time when they thought I was going to die. My grandmother said I was falling asleep, and they couldn't wake me up. They cut me to wake me up."

"Dianne is hot tempered like her father – she is the only feisty one in the family," says Tô. "She was always a good student. She never gave us any worries growing up. She can handle herself."

"Dianne was a very compliant child," says Thiêu. "It is the truth. She was good at school. Asian children are told to be compliant with their elders. Education is different between Asian and Western society.

"The Eastern way is about a hierarchy of respect. You are taught to respect your elders and your teachers, respect the police and authority. How it is carried out on a personal level is different. If Western kids have a dispute with their parents, it is up to their parents to defend their position. In Asian society, even if parents are wrong, children don't say anything. We kept that when we came to Australia, and although Dianne questioned us often, she never disobeyed us."

Dianne said that there are certain things she would question but wouldn't think of going against her parent's wishes.

The Kids

"I would question things to validate them in my mind," she says. "I was trying to determine my own values. I understood the fealty between the family, and the mother and the father and that positional arena where they are one step ahead of you in terms of what is going on around you, and you have to listen to them."

Dianne ended up marrying Tony and they had three children, Kenneth, Teagan and Anabelle. In 2024 Kenneth married Loan Nguyen. Tony and Dianne ended up buying and selling several pharmacies, before going into partnership with a few other pharmacists. Between them, they run three pharmacies in western Sydney. Dianne and Tony divorced more than six years ago (at the time of writing of this book), but there parting was cordial, and they remain business partners. As well as having financial interests in the pharmacies, Dianne started a new career as a social worker in 2024 after graduating with a master's in social work in 2023.

Being the youngest and maybe having the foresight of seeing any pitfalls her sisters and brother fell into and avoiding them, Joanne has led the least tumultuous life of the four siblings. She was the only member of the family to marry outside of the Asian culture, having been married to her South African-born Australian husband Jan, for the best part of 20 years.

They have a set of twin girls – Caitlin and Martine – and a son, Liam. Like Dianne, she owned and ran a pharmacy, but once the children came along, became more of a stay-at-home mother until the children reached an age where she could go back out into the workforce.

For all the ups and downs that life has thrown at Thiêu and Tô, they are glad they did what they did. They feel they made the right decisions, and that they and their descendants have benefited from those decisions made in rural Viêtnam almost five decades ago.

A Packet of Cigarettes

"We made the right choice to come," says Thiêu. "This country has given us opportunities we never would have had in Viêtnam, and we will always be grateful for that."

Chapter 22

The Children's Stories

Jennifer's Story (Bich Nhi) – Eldest Daughter/First Child

I HAVE SO MANY LASTING MEMORIES OF VIÊTNAM. Most of them are also of my sister Dianne as we were so close in age.

When I was really young, Dianne and I lived with our grandparents, my aunty and her two children. The elder one, Trúóng Thuc Linh, was a girl who looked after me, while her younger brother, Trúóng Van Chan, looked after Dianne. It was like we were on two different teams – we were partners for everything – from tutorials to playing games, from acting out scenes from shows through to sword fights, and then sneaking out for dessert between meals, or we would just simply hang out.

It was Team Older versus Team Younger. Team Older always got to be the heroes because the eldest person said so, which

A Packet of Cigarettes

meant Team Younger had to be the villains. Of course, the villains always had to die at the end. Dianne often disputed why they had to always be the villains, to which our eldest cousin explained Team Older didn't know how to be the villains. I remember Dianne was never happy when she was defeated even though she died each time and still played along.

When we were a little older, we went and lived with my mum and her older brother, my uncle. My dad was not around as he had to work away from home. Mum and my uncle worked seven days a week, so we were looked after by a servant. Dianne and I were never allowed out of the house so we used to sit behind our corrugated iron door waiting for the two little boys next door who could leave their house to come over and play with us. We passed things back and forth through the little openings of the corrugated door.

I recall that I was very scared whenever Mum went to work, and I would cry but I can't remember why. It was only in my 50s that I understood. Mum told me that while we were living at that house, on one occasion, she returned home 15 minutes after she left for work because she forgot something. She found the hired help holding me upside down by my feet and dunking me head-first into the ceramic water storage pot. This lady was asked to leave immediately.

I remembered a few accidents that left their scars on me. Like the one on my knee from the time I fell out of a taxi. Luckily, my mum held on to me, so it was only my right knee that scraped along the road. There was another scrap on one of my ankles from when it was caught in the chain of a bike as I was trying to find a place to rest my foot.

Then there was the time Dianne, and I got in trouble with the police. When Dianne was in kindergarten and I was in Year One, we walked from our Chinese school to Mum's shop. It was very close, but we had to walk through a public garden

The Children's Stories

to get there. Dianne and I saw these beautiful flowers, so we excitedly picked a few. A policemen came up to us, took our hands and asked us where we lived. We were very scared, and I told him that our Mum's shop was nearby. He took us there and told Mum that if we picked flowers from the public park again, we would be fined. He let us off with the warning. Mum scolded us in front of him and when we got home, we had to kneel as a punishment.

We were soon joined by my brother Chris. Chris was slow to speak. He didn't start speaking until he was three. My parents thought he was mute. He didn't have any passion to speak but he was very passionate about food. He would climb up the bed so he could reach a bundle of tiny bananas, and he ate most of them when everyone was busy. Chris had all sorts of strategies when he hunted for food around the house. However, there was one time we heard him scream and cry loudly. We found him with his finger stuck between the lid and the edge of the tin of condensed milk.

Most of the time, Dianne and I were each other's companions. We kept each other entertained. We were creative and kept each other busy with games and songs we made up. Dianne and I would keep certain fruit seeds that we could peel the exterior skin off after we ate.

After we peeled them, we would play with them and create games around them. We had a lot of fun with these seeds. We took turns to flick them to see who can get closest to the skirting board without touching it. We threw them one by one at the wall to see who can rebound the furthest. We also washed them and put them in our mouth and shoot them out to see who could shoot further. Chris wanted to join, and I said no because I figured he would just swallow it. Dianne and I then decided to up the challenge so we washed these seeds and put them in one of our nostrils to shoot them to see who can shoot further.

A Packet of Cigarettes

While we were busy laughing, we didn't pay any attention to Chris. The next thing we knew, Chris was crying and sticking his first finger up his nose. We laid him down and pulled his finger out and saw that he'd one of our seeds shoved up his nose. We took him downstairs as he was crying, and my dad was horrified. He desperately tried to suck the seed out of Chris's nose but couldn't, so they took him to the doctor to get it removed. Dianne and I got caned – one on each hand – and were told never to play with seeds again.

My lasting memories of Viêtnam are of my early childhood. I was an awkward child with low self-esteem yet had a great sense of responsibility for my siblings. I also struggled at school and didn't really have any close friends. I remembered I couldn't identify with my classmates or understand them. I was not happy at school.

Dianne was an outgoing, confident, able child who seemed to naturally assimilate. She had friends and there was always that special girl who was her best friend. She enjoyed school and did well. We were very disciplined, well-behaved children. Well, except for my crazy creative ideas that got us into trouble from time to time, Dianne's curiosity and Chris' passion for food.

The first time we tried to leave Viêtnam, it was unsuccessful. I remembered it was very dark, and we had to walk towards the water. We walked off the road, then onto dry ground, then suddenly, we were ankle deep in mud. We all lost our shoes in the mud but kept moving.

Mum carried Joanne who was about nine months old and held onto Chris with her other hand. She told me to hold Dianne's hand and stay close to her. Whatever happens, she said, even if I lose her, I cannot let go of Dianne's hand. It was so dark and so many people were moving, it was hard to see so I held onto her shirt from the back with my other hand. We got on a small boat, where we sat quietly with some elderly

The Children's Stories

people. People were shining torches around looking for their shoes in the mud, which made everyone nervous. They must have thought that it was only a matter of time before the authorities would arrive, so they abandoned the plan, and we went home before sunrise.

The second attempt was successful. It was from this trip on that my dad was a constant figure in our lives. Before stepping on this fishing boat, Dad was a person that we saw randomly every now and then. It didn't bother me that we didn't see him that often because I thought this was the same for everyone. My siblings and I didn't really have a close relationship with my parents when we were younger because Dad was working away from home and Mum was working seven days a week, which meant that when she got home, she was tired.

When we left the second time, Mum told Dianne and I that we are going to a wedding. We were both very excited. We had never been to a wedding before, so we spent days fantasising about the event. On the actual day, we were taken to a dinghy, which took us out to a bigger boat where Dad was waiting for us. When we boarded, we were taken to an undercover area of the boat and were told to keep quiet. I remembered asking Mum where the wedding was and if we were going there by boat. She said to keep quiet. After what seemed like a long time we came up. I was exhausted and felt seasick, Dianne was sleeping, and there was no wedding.

When we arrived at the refugee camp in Malaysia, the refugees would run out to see if there is anyone they knew. My uncle's friend saw us, so he brought us instant noodles. My dad and others then built a massive tent for us all to stay there on the beach that first night.

We only stayed at the refugee camp for two months before we were told we would be going to Australia.

A Packet of Cigarettes

Mum and Dad made the right decision to leave. It would not have been an easy decision, but once they decided, we had to go. Such decisions require a lot of courage, support and understanding. Their motivation was to give their children the best opportunities possible, to have a better life, a brighter future. However, they had chosen a different set of life challenges for themselves and their children.

They chose to step forward into a world of uncertainty empty handed. They chose to start over again. They had to rebuild their lives with four very young children depending on them. I don't believe they understood how much of a disadvantage they would have due to the impact of the language barrier. They also could not have anticipated the wide cultural gap between Viêtnam and Australia, or the sacrifices that we all had to make over the years.

We each battled the challenges of life in our own way, to the best of our abilities. We were blessed and did not perish at sea like many did, so we knew we had to make our sacrifices count. We not only survive but thrive. We must make our efforts worthwhile.

The turning point in my life was my arranged marriage to Van in Perth. I went from a child who never dated into a marriage, where one of the first things I asked my mother was, "How do I know I love this person?"

She replied, "The longer you stay with him, the more you love him."

I was not prepared for it, and I became terribly homesick being stuck in Perth. Family values and culture are so important to me, and even though Van and I were both culturally Viêtnamese, our values were different. It was very difficult to fall in love with someone whom I had very little in common with and much harder still to be married to someone I found difficult to respect.

The Children's Stories

It was at this point that I realised not only that Eastern and Western cultures are different, but Asian families can be different, too. I realised I'd lived a sheltered life and that I was ignorant of many facets of what was going on around me. We were taught to be kind and giving, so I assumed everyone was like this. We were never taught to be assertive or to protect ourselves, which meant during my marriage, I became emotionally and mentally scarred from being used, abused and exploited.

I worked 13 hours a day, seven days a week from the time I was married and through both of my pregnancies up until each time I gave birth. I was given a month off to rest and recover, then expected to resume work. Everything was so overwhelming. I didn't realise that I had an uncaring, unloving husband who wasn't ready to be a husband and a father, even though he was six years my senior.

We were the first in both of our families to be married. I was so miserable with many areas of my life due to our values not being aligned. Regardless of how depressed I was, I thought this is marriage, everyone is dealing with the same thing, so I kept soldiering on.

I tried to discuss my feelings with my husband to which he said, "Just ignore the things that aren't right, be a good person, and forgive my family members when you feel they have wronged you."

Basically, just do what he does because self-sacrifice for family peace is more important. I didn't see the rest of the family follow those rules and these rules only seemed to apply to him and I. He was okay that I frequently cried to sleep at night only to wake up every morning knowing that more mental and emotional anguish was waiting.

It wasn't until my husband's sister and then Dianne got married that I slowly saw that other husbands were caring, loving, kind, and thoughtful to their wives and their wives' needs. They protected their wives and once they had their child, they took care of them. My brother-in-law would take my sister-in-law home early if she was tired. I remembered thinking how lucky she was.

Whenever I was dizzy from morning sickness, my husband told me to go to the warehouse and lie on a pallet of rice bags for a little while then go back to work. I didn't challenge any of this behaviour because I assumed that this is how they treat pregnant women in their family.

As my married life unravelled, the more I saw how cruel life really could be. It was sad when I saw his family as my own, but they saw me as free labour. I was so depressed my body was crying out for a break. I was on 20 tablets a day to address my heart and thyroid issues, my migraines and my mental state. Those six years were the most challenging time of my life. For the struggles that I endured, I was gifted with two beautiful, kind daughters for which I am forever grateful.

The third turning point was when I met Joseph. He was the opposite of my ex-husband. He was smart, driven, kind, mindful, independent, and thoughtful towards my daughters and I. He was my friend, my companion, my teacher, my business partner, my financial supporter, my children's father figure and my life partner for 19 years. He taught me many life and business skills. In turn, I was his sounding board when it came to work. Even today, we still trust, care for and respect each other's needs. We motivate and inspire each other. We support each other's dreams and aspirations.

Joseph's brother Johnny introduced us. Joseph brought his daughter Mikayla to the family, and I brought Sarah and Stephanie. We did consider trying for a son but when he ran the idea past five-year-old Mikayla, she said, "No."

Over the years, the girls got along well, and we were a nice family until Mikayla passed away three months before her

The Children's Stories

18th birthday. Joseph was devastated. He missed his daughter terribly and deep down; he had the desire to have another child. I was too old to give him a child.

I offered to move out when he found a new life partner who could fulfil his wishes and ensure that he had another child. He or she should wake up happy every day knowing their parents were in the next room. I made choices that may not make sense to others, but they made sense to me.

If we had remained in Viêtnam, my dad would have chosen my career. Not wanting to disappoint my parents, I would have followed. He often told me that he was going to teach me photography so I could take annual photos for private girls' schools as well as international schools. I would probably still have gotten married, had kids and conformed to society. I believe my values may be different as my experiences and perceptions of life would have been different. I don't believe I would have as much freedom as I do now to live life on my own terms. I would certainly not be as courageous in my approach to life, work or social affairs.

Viêtnam's culture encourages, supports and prioritises men's learning and development over women. Life would probably have been more hectic, and opportunities would have been more competitive. Even if my personal life was great, Viêtnam is still considered a third-world country compared to Australia. The differences between the countries weren't just economic, but also reflected in the population's mindset, attitude, behaviour, culture, etc, which would contribute to our experiences and our perception and therefore shape our lives.

It had always been challenging and confusing to live and conduct life with Eastern values while living in a Western society. This was a time when Westerners knew little about Asian culture, food and values. I grew up in my early years struggling to belong. Eastern and Western values were

A Packet of Cigarettes

conflicting most of the time. I found it hard to achieve some sort of responsibility towards my family as I strived to be the best daughter possible to alleviate my parent's stress because I could see they were working so hard. I had to make sure I looked after my siblings. Dianne was always next to me as second in command. I came up with the ideas and how we should carry out tasks and she would help me execute them.

Upon reflection, we were children who ended up taking care of children from the time we stepped on Malaysian soil. We didn't have a choice; we had to be a good team, and we had to make it work.

My father was very strict. He had been in the army so if we didn't do as we were told, he would make us hold our ears and squat down all the way and stand up. We had to do this many times. If we did something bad, then we would be caned on our hands. If we were arguing or fighting, then we knelt first while we waited for him to discipline us, then we would lie face down and be caned on our backside.

Joanne was too young to know anything, but she still knelt and lied down, but she didn't get caned. Chris rarely got caned because he was young and only followed the leaders. Dianne got caned when we both took responsibility for whatever mistakes had been made. I was caned the most because I was the eldest and should have known better. I thought it's a given that after kids are born, especially the eldest ones, they just know things naturally. I used to feel bad not knowing things.

I remember both my parents worked in the factory in the afternoon shift, which meant they started at about 2pm and didn't get home till about 1:30am. Chris had started kindergarten, so Dianne and I took him together when we walked to school and back. Joanne was two-and-a-half, so she had to stay at home by herself from the time our parents left at 2pm until we rushed home from school at 3:20pm. Mum

The Children's Stories

put a potty in the corner and told Joanne if she needed to pee then go there. The television was turned on to some cartoon channel, while a few biscuits, a bottle of milk and a bottle of water were on the table. She also left a blanket and pillow on the floor. When we arrived home, we went to the window and called out Joanne's name. Joanne was too small to open the door, so she ran into the room, climbed onto the bed and lifted the latch to open the window. Dianne and I would push Chris into the window, and he was tall enough to open the door for us. We got in, played, coloured in our colouring-in books, and ate the food Mum prepared for dinner. I showered Chris and Joanne, then Dianne and I also showered, and we all would continue to watch television.

I remembered we used to love watching *Scooby Doo, Josie and The Pussy Cats, The Flintstones, I Dream of Jeannie, The Bionic Woman, Bewitched, The Brady Bunch, The Ghost and Mrs Muir, Monkey Magic, Charlie's Angels* and of course, my favourite, *Wonder Woman* . Not only did we watch these shows, but we also each took on the different characters and would run around the lounge acting out different parts. We didn't have toys or puzzles, or parents to keep us company. The shows on television accompanied us, subsequently teaching us that good always defeats evil.

Western culture encourages children to share personal thoughts and challenging questions, whereas Eastern cultures tell us to be quiet unless we are spoken to. We are also never to challenge or ask questions or speak back to an adult. It is considered rude and uncultured. Going to school with Eastern values meant I was not taking part in class. Going home with behavioural teachings from there landed me in trouble. My siblings seemed to find a way to cope while I struggled all through school and beyond. Throughout my school years, I never felt happy or that I belonged anywhere. I found a few

A Packet of Cigarettes

nice people that I called friends in high school, but I was still awkward and lost.

After I finished my schooling, I thought life would be simpler, but it was not. In Western culture, it is normal for any 18-year-old to go out with friends, have boyfriends, and travel. However, in our family, it wasn't good to go out with boys or with friends. I was encouraged to be a responsible adult and to not be seen with boys because it would ruin my reputation. If that happened, it would result in doom and gloom for all my siblings. So, I stepped out of high school and walked into my family's photography business where my dad drove me to work and home seven days a week, 12 hours a day. I saw other people my age go out to parties or hang out with friends.

During the 1980s, young Australians moved out of home as soon as they were old enough whereas Asian kids stayed at home until they were married. I found that Australians were not as focused on self-sacrifice as first-generation Asian refugees. We had nothing, so each generation must achieve something and be a stepping stone for the next. There was no fairness, or indulgence, only sacrifice until we achieved more than the generation before us.

When it comes to money, Western culture is clearcut and everyone takes care of their own personal affairs. Asians are the opposite. They would lend their money back and forth to help each other buy properties, or when going through tough times.

When it comes to gifts, Western culture encourages thoughtful gifts as it expresses how well a person knows another's like and dislikes. Asians believe that the best gift is money in a lucky red pouch.

Western culture teaches us to look after ourselves first, and when our cup is full and we are strong enough, we then look

The Children's Stories

after our family. In contrast, Asians are considered selfish if they don't sacrifice themselves.

Western culture teaches us to spend and reward ourselves because we deserve it. We should go on holiday because we've worked hard all year and deserve a break. You can revisit a destination if you love it. Whatever assets are left for the kids is a bonus. Asian culture teaches us to work and save. Save as much as we can for our children and grandchildren. Don't waste money, always look for a bargain because why pay more when you don't have to? You don't need to go back to a destination as it is unnecessary and a waste of money. That money is best spent elsewhere.

When it comes to education, Westerners are more relaxed as they place importance on getting the job they enjoy. Asians will throw money for tutorials, private schools, whatever it takes to gain that completive edge. Achievement of most facets, except sports, of their children's education is important. With so many contradictions, it's a wonder many Asians in Western cultures suffer from mental health issues.

Family is very important to me. I was taught very early on in life my responsibilities towards my family. With all my struggles, I still managed to be a responsible, mindful daughter to my parents, a caring and thoughtful sister to my siblings, a loving fulfilling person to my life partner. I feel okay with all my relationships within my family except for my role as a parent; the most challenging thing I've found in life is motherhood.

I struggled to be the kind of mother that my children deserved. Now that we are all adults, we need more space and time to process our personal perspectives of our past, as well as understand ourselves better before we can try to understand each other better. We love, care and respect each other. We make very little demands and give as much support and share as much joy as we can. Things are getting better, and I am very proud of my big girl, baby, and myself. I am working on being a mother they feel lucky to have in their adult years.

Growing up, suffering from so many emotional, mental, and physical traumas, I suffered from severe mental health issues and struggled to provide a safe and healthy environment for my children. My children and I did the best we could to manoeuvre through some of the conflicting values and ideals between east and west.

Western parents encourage a close friendship with their children and respect their life decisions. Once grown, their children are adults and have equal rights as their parents. However, when they are young, we must prioritise their needs and protect them. We must listen to our children, and if our children are playing up, we must understand why and help them resolve it. Western parents are happy as long as their children are happy regardless of academic and sporting achievements. They don't care how well they do house chores, accumulate assets, and their physical appearance. They encourage their children to be themselves and be extraordinary.

However, Asian parents suggest it's best to keep a distance and clear boundaries for each generation to ensure children respect older adults. Young people must always compromise and prioritise the needs of older people. Kids must listen to their parents; if they play up and don't obey then they must be disciplined. Asian parents are expected to teach and guide their children towards success. Parents are judged based on their children's achievements.

Asian parents place more importance on the achievements of their children than the happiness of their children. Asian parents like their children to blend in and be ordinary. It's great not to attract attention – stay under the radar so people don't know much about you.

The Children's Stories

As for my personal journey, I have suffered. I tried giving up with three suicide attempts. Then I decided to fight. I have persevered through the toughest of times, and I have cried more times than I smiled. I have grieved, I have celebrated the many turning points of my life, and I now focus on self-care and self-love. I also encourage and support my children to do the same; as long as we are all healthy and happy, I am satisfied.

Regardless of my suffering, I am grateful to my parents who did their best with what they had. It is okay that they are not perfect, just as it is okay that I am far from perfect. I live, I learn, I accept, I forgive, I care, I love. I choose a life of less judgement. I choose to have the courage to design and create a life of fulfilment and possibilities.

Life...is all a matter of perspective.

Dianne's Story (Tuyet Nhi) – Second Daughter/Second Child

My memory of Viêtnam is a bit sketchy; I remember feeling a bit trapped as Jennifer and I weren't allowed outside to play with the neighbouring children. We were kept inside and watched the world from our sleeping quarters. We would spend many hours acting out different stories, people watching and making up stories about them and sometimes Jennifer would play teacher where she taught me and our carer (live-in nanny) the alphabet and numbers. When Chris arrived, there was just an extra student in our "class" and one more extra we could add to our stories.

The trip over to Malaysia was uneventful in my memory, too. I did remember trying to eat this terrible boiled fish and was thankful for the commotion as we were being rushed off

A Packet of Cigarettes

the boat, being passed from uncle to uncle to get us onto the shores close to Kuala Terrenganu. We spent the rest of the day swimming on the beach and that night we slept on the beach. The days in Malaysia were idyllic – Jennifer and I would watch over our siblings and little cousins while the adults attended to more pressing matters.

Our trip to Australia was highly anticipated. We spent many days imagining what our new home would look like and what food we would indulge in because our destination had been painted in our minds as a place of Nirvana. No war, no poverty and no threats. This was affirmed when our plane landed on Christmas Eve 1977 and the next day, we all received a present from Santa. To a little girl who had just spent the last three months at sea and on an island living in a refugee camp, this was truly heaven. We all felt we were the luckiest people in the world.

Growing up in a new land proved challenging as our parents grappled with the new country, learning English, getting a job, navigating the community and keeping us safe. They were absent often. Because we were close in age, Jennifer and I were given the dual responsibilities as pseudo parents to our younger siblings Chris and Joanne. We would both wear the accolades if we got it right and the punishment if we got it wrong. Jennifer could outrank me as she was the eldest and therefore usually had the final call. To a young girl though, I felt she took advantage of this position and changed the goal post whenever she saw fit... I wasn't happy about that!

As children we all seek approval from our parents. How the pie of affirmation is divided will vary between families – with our family, it was through accolades. Thinking back on it now, I wonder whether this was a good strategy or not. I learnt the rules of the game fast, and I snared a large part of my dad's approval. My dad often spoke proudly about my academic and sporting achievements. I was a little girl trying to find her place and identity in this world. I didn't really have the complete picture, I just wanted to please my parents.

I often wondered about my parents' strict ways and the Eastern philosophy of collectivism, had it hampered our growth? I now reflect on how difficult it must have been for my siblings. How Joanne must have felt learning to be quiet around the noise of her elder siblings leading the way when she may have wanted to contribute more but didn't think it was her place to do so. How difficult it might have been for Chris to be his authentic self and live his truth as a gay man and be accepted and loved as himself and not judged by what he could bring to his family. For Jennifer, how difficult it must have been to find her true authentic self when she's busy trying to appease our parents with all their requests and expectations which led to limited opportunities to explore her own needs. I watched helplessly and tried ineffectively to help. Who did we become to make it all work?

Although the 'White Australia' policy to immigration was abolished in 1975, Dad's maverick move to Penrith in 1980s caused me a lot of angst. Along with normal teenage insecurities, we had strict parents with old fashion values surrounding dating and sex. Then there was the bullying because the demographics in Penrith at the time did not include ethnic diversity so fitting in and running with the crowd was difficult. I even found myself in a hair pulling fight with one of the "tough kids" one afternoon because she thought I was an easy target.

I don't know if it was a desire to be less obtrusive so that I wasn't targeted by bullies, or my desire to win more favours from my parents that I made the decision to throw myself into the school curriculum and study hard. I managed to be dux of my year a couple of times and eventually had a mark that allowed me to study for a Bachelor of Pharmacy – a goal set for me by my parents.

The Eastern vs Western philosophy in family expectations, the patriarchal nuances of Eastern values and the martyrdom imposed on many Asian women did not sit too well with me. The onus on 'happy family' was usually placed on the mother of the family. She is usually the nurturer, the carer, the cook and cleaner. What do you do when you do not possess these qualities? I felt I was ill-equipped with empathy or nurturing as I didn't have the opportunity to develop them. Most of my developmental years were focused on survival and achievements.

My marriage came to an end in 2015. One of my close friends, Diep, had passed away from breast cancer and after much retrospection and reflection, I had accepted that this life is not a dress rehearsal and that my current priorities were not authentic. After many failed attempts to try and engage my ex-husband to couples therapy, I made the heart aching decision to listen to my inner voice to search for my spiritual and authentic self and to find my life's purpose by going solo. My biggest fears were the impact that a divorce may have on my children.

This was my biggest leap of faith. My saving grace was that there seem to be modest damage (that I can see anyway) to the psychological, emotional, and financial state of everyone involved – him, my children and myself. Both my ex and I looked for win-win solutions while we were trying to untangle our marriage. We tried to leave our emotions at the door while we tried and discuss fair and equitable strategies around the kitchen table. It required a fair, unbiased mediator in the name of Kenneth, our eldest son. My children continue to be the three best things that I have been blessed with.

My years being single before I met my partner Mike were the most instrumental years of my self-awareness journey. Not

The Children's Stories

having to place my parent's needs or my family's needs ahead of my own, I followed the self-care mantra where I prioritised my own needs first. The open space, reflective thinking, mindfulness practice and engagement of a personal coach helped me gather more pieces to my puzzle and the picture became clearer.

When Mike came into my world, I was already a more complete woman, ready to learn, give and receive affection. Mike is not deterred by my aggressive temperament when I'm in Alpha-woman mode; he placates me and picks his battles on a different day. Slowly the hard, rough exterior has been replaced by softer edges. I continue to grow and evolve; I hope that in 20 years' time, we are deeper in love with each other and more accepting of ourselves.

Completing my Master of Social Work and becoming a mental health social worker was another major change that gave me the knowledge and insight of family trauma and all the personal traumas (some big, some small) that my family endured as we resettled in Australia after the war.

Through the social worker lens, the difficulties experienced by refugee families were highlighted. I had the skills and information to retrospect understand many past family traumas that we all experienced due to the difficult circumstances we found ourselves in. I'm working hard to address my traumas and hold space for others who crosses my path. I'm forever grateful to my parents, knowing that they have given us their absolute best and I will give my utmost effort trying to live out my father's dying wish; to always take care of one and other. Family is everything – even the imperfect ones.

A Packet of Cigarettes

Chris' Story (Nhut Tan) – Only Son/Third Child

I would've been five years old when we left Viêtnam, so I think my memories have been formed through hearing the retelling of certain events on the voyage and pictures.

I do remember vividly the night that we were waiting to be picked up by the canoe that would take us out to the fishing trawler. It was cold and damp and I was being eaten alive by mosquitoes. My orders were to remain silent and not make any noise, which was difficult until my auntie comforted me by letting me play with her ears. I find ears soothing.

I also recall on the night being very cold while our vessel made its way past the guards at various checkpoints. I was told later that my dad had stowed everyone in the hull of the boat where he kept blocks of ice for the fish that he caught.

As for the journey itself, I don't remember much. We bumped into other fishermen who came onboard to ask my dad if he had ice to spare. They'd run out of ice and needed some to prevent their abundant catch from spoiling. My dad exchanged his blocks of ice and in return they gave us some fresh fish.

I also remember there was a piercing pain to my inner thigh. My aunty had pinched me there and I shrieked and cried. I learned later that Dad had given the instruction to all the mothers on board who was carrying an infant to make them cry so that our fisherman guest would leave our vessel. The next thing I remember is us landing on the shores of Malaysia.

At the time, you didn't think about having to straddle two different cultures. My dad's ethos with regard to Australia was simple – we come to a new country, and to survive, we must adapt and assimilate.

We moved out west where housing was affordable, and my siblings and I assimilated to the Aussie culture. But in doing so, we were also less in-tune with our Asian culture. It's

The Children's Stories

only in more recent years that I'm trying to reconnect with my Viêtnamese heritage. As a child, I resented the question, "Where are you from?" or "Where were you born?" because I was ashamed of the fact that we were refugees to this country. Today, I wear that badge proudly.

Coming out as gay in 1993 was an interesting experience and is still a work in progress. My dad had faced countless challenges, problems and obstacles in his life and that always found a way to navigate through, around, solve or resolve. I believe my coming out presented him with the biggest headache. Finally, a problem that my dad could not make go away. He didn't kick me out of family, which was common in our culture during the early 90s, but he couldn't hide his disappointment and shame I had brought into the family.

In his own way, my dad did accept me and my new 'lifestyle choices', but I knew my sexuality completely stumped him. If I could sum up the timeline of my dad's acceptance of my sexuality, it would look like this:

1993: Shock, family tries to get me to church to 'pray the gay away'. 1994-2008: Years where I wanted to go unnoticed during my family gatherings. My immediate family knew I was gay, but curious cousins, aunties and uncles also start probing myself and my parents about my relationship status. The default line that 'Chris is single, he's not dating' no longer appeased my extended family. I withdrew from some of my family's gatherings. I didn't want to constantly be answering questions about my personal life.

2009-2024: Evolution of acceptance. I guess the change began in 2009. This was the year that my dad agreed to meet my partner. It was at our immediate family gathering. It was a quick handshake and a 'hello', but it meant so much to me.

Over the years, my dad got better at accepting my homosexuality; it was a slow burn. It took years to smooth out the bumps and lines on his journey to acceptance. I know it wasn't easy for him, but true to form, he never gave up.

Joanne's Story (Tu Nhi) – Youngest Daughter/Fourth Child

I think growing up, the pressure for me trying to straddle two different cultures was relieved by having older siblings. I was shielded from the early years of adjusting to new cultures, having to hold on to the one we left behind. There wasn't much expectation to 'know' much. This, coupled with being the youngest in the family, meant that I didn't have much of a voice, and I didn't mind this one bit.

Culturally, I found myself following trodden paths when it came to adjusting to a new school in an area that was very white. I remember that Mum and Dad generally said no to most social events that I wanted to attend, but if my sister Dianne gave them the nod of approval, then things would look up.

As an adult, more was expected of me, but learning and appreciating cultural norms was not a straightforward passing down of knowledge. I learned it through a combination of watching other families, trial and error and accepting I would never have cultural fluency.

My husband, Jan, is Western. He emigrated to Australia from South Africa when he was 10. By the time I started dating Jan, I had already had one serious relationship with someone who was a closer cultural fit. When that ended, it was all downhill for me. Bringing home anyone who was employed and didn't have a gambling or drinking problem was going to be better than the life of eternal spinsterhood that my parents were preparing themselves for.

The Children's Stories

Mum kept warning me that the more people I dated, the less of a catch I would be to a prospective husband. This is a hang up from the old culture that they hadn't left behind – that one's virtue and worthiness was tied to one's reputation, which was very closely linked to perceived purity.

In other words, once you start dating someone, you must marry as soon as practical before they grow tired of you and find another partner and marry them instead. The more times you entered this cycle, the less likely you are to secure a marriage. You can imagine their joy when Jan proposed.

I really enjoyed visiting Viêtnam with my parents. I had visited before but stayed in the city and tourist spots. The trip in 2010 was just amazing as it felt like Mum and Dad were finally able to take us back and show us the best bits of their homeland; how they passed the time, family they supported, friends they kept in contact with and food they enjoyed. They wanted to show us off to their relatives too.

I remember observing those around me. People my age, people younger than me. I was grateful that my life was different. Like Dianne, having an opportunity to get a pharmaceutical degree at university and become a professional was not accessible to most in Bac Lieu, my parents' hometown.

I wondered what my life would have been like, who would I have married (choices seemed very limited, and spinsters aplenty)? What would my children have done? Would I have resented the likes of someone like me, with a life of plenty? I'm glad Dad and Mum made the choice to leave Viêtnam to find a better life for us all.

Epilogue

On July 28th, 2024, at 9.05pm Thiêu Cao passed away peacefully at the Royal Brisbane and Women's Hospital in Brisbane, Queensland surrounded by Tô, his children and grandchildren. He had been on holiday with Tô and Jennifer visiting his nephew.

Early in the morning of the 26th, he suffered a stroke, having spent the previous evening singing karaoke and dancing with Tô and the rest of his extended family.

By the evening of the 26th, he rallied and seemed to be on his way to recovery, only to suffer a massive stroke on the morning of July 27th from which he never recovered.

Dianne's Epilogue

On a recent trip to Việtnam in November 2024, I was overwhelmed with sadness when my flight landed in Saigon. Having made this trip numerous times, this flight was sentimental as it was my first trip after Dad's passing.

I imagined how my father must have felt when he made the decision in 1977 to leave behind everything he had ever known. To gamble his life and those of his loved ones for the chance of freedom. Being lost at sea was a possible outcome, in surviving that, re-establishing a new life would bring with it other challenges. His reasoning to us was that each generation should be able to make sacrifices to ensure "greener pastures" for the next generation.

As readers of this biography of Mr Thieu Cao, I'm going to assume that you are somehow related to him, or you came from a similar journey across the Pacific Ocean after the war. The purpose of this book is to leave behind family history of a significant forefather.

You may never have to be at a point in your life where you have to make decision that might mean life or death for you and your family; but I'm sure the challenges you face will seem just as difficult or just as heart-wrenching. Just remember the values that my father always embraced: integrity, determination and family.

Let these values guide and inspire to decide to turn left or right, to embrace the freedom you were born into and work hard to protect it.

Those are the blessed who have access to choice.

Appendix

The Children's Eulogies to Thiêu

Jennifer

Dad, I know you are here with us.
Dad, I know you can hear us.
Thank you for being my father.

Dad, walking through the house knowing that I won't see you again brings hundreds of memories flooding into my mind. The pain in my heart brings tears to my eyes.

Dad, I miss the things you say, the things you do, your laughter, the jokes you made and of course your expression of love and care through acts of service.

Dad, your relationship with Mum is one that inspired many. I remembered when I was young while thinking about my future, I always wish I could find someone similar to you.

A Packet of Cigarettes

Your deep love, joy, connection, support and understanding with Mum over the years aspire us to keep working, improving our own relationships as you and Mum have shown us the way with some efforts.

Dad, I walked into your bedroom and looking at your side of the bed I saw Mum dressed up your long pillow under the quilt. It allows her to talk to you, remembering your conversations and say good morning and good night to you. I can see how much she misses you in her own private safe space. I know you both love each other dearly.

Dad, the dining table where we share many happy meals together. Mum still has your bowl of rice and chopsticks during mealtime. I still feel your presence.

Dad, the keyboard is where you unleash your creativities and play for Mum and friends to sing and dance to. I can still hear the music.

Dad, the table tennis where you and Mum sweated out is half empty. I still remember how you patiently taught me table tennis. I still remembered you laughing saying I didn't have potential at table tennis like your mum.

Dad, the lounge where you sit or lie to watch the TV every day, a place where I said, "Hey Dad," most often is now empty. This room will never be the same.

Dad, the garden that you tend to, the fruits and vegetables just like us are still here missing you touching our lives, but you are nowhere to be seen. We miss you so dearly.

I never realised how often I call out Dad! If something need fixing... Dad. Can't find something... Dad. Something not working... Dad. Looking for Mum... Dad. Not sure about something... Dad. Unsure about cooking something... Dad.

I miss you, Dad. I miss the fact that I can no longer call out Dad but only silently in my heart call Dad.

The Children's Eulogies to Thiêu

Dad, your children have pieces of you, your grandchildren have fragments of you. You have been a gem of a husband, a loving, caring father and grandfather.

You have done a great job. You showed us that we can create any kind of life we want if we have the courage and spirit to persevere. Yes, just like you... Yes, even with very a humble beginning. You made your mark in this world, and we will follow the trail of footprints you left behind.

Dad, be proud, be happy, be peaceful, be free. Fly to heaven, I know you will continue to look over our family.

Pa, pa vui ve nhe nhang len thiên đường phu ho cho mum va gia Dinh minh luon lion manh khoe.

Dianne, Chris, Joanne and I will take care of Mum and of each other and our children, just as always.

Dad, we love you dearly. Dad, we miss you dearly. Dad, we take comfort in the memories you left us in our hearts and remember your teachings in our head. Dad, forever you will be in our hearts.

Dianne

As far as I can remember, my father was my *Superman*. He was the person that had all the answers, protected us and kept us safe. I idolised him and wanted to walk in his footsteps, his validation and affirmation were paramount in my formative years. I took on so many of his traits, some good, some not so good.

About a year ago, an acquaintance who had recently met my father made an observation that, "This man must be born of nobility, how he thinks, acts and holds himself is admirable."

She may have been jesting with my parents as she could be reciprocating my dad's great sense of humour. Nonetheless, my parents chuckled at the comment because they both knew the inner story.

An amazing story that compelled my partner and I to want to write a biography about him. It saddens me that we didn't quite get *A Packet of Cigarettes* completed for him in his living years. However, I gained so much insight into him as a person and my parents as a couple as we wiled away the afternoons with them sharing their life's adventures. I gained much more reverence for him through adult eyes. Our hope is that this book will serve its purpose by reminding our children, grandchildren and future generations his extraordinary human spirit. It is as much a life story as a love story about two people supporting each other, building a family, surviving war, overcoming adversities in a foreign country and living a life of servitude and self- sacrifice.

My dad was orphaned at the age of four due to unfortunate circumstances. Growing up in rural Viêtnam, where money, family and societal connection ensured an easier passage to life, my father had none. The difficulties that he confronted as he moved through life, did not kill him, it absolutely made him stronger. He was not an educated man, yet his critical thinking nature and thoughtful reasoning helped him select righteous, wholesome and virtuous values for himself to become that "noble gentleman" this lady thought he was.

I think back on my parents throughout the years, and I can see how committed and loving relationships are forged. There was devotion, restraint and merging of two lives into one. Theirs is a relationship that people admire and try to emulate.

One of his other lessons was to stay open to learning; he was constantly refining his processes. He may have had his personal flaws but towards the end of his life, his hard exterior fell away, his raison d'etre was only to be accountable to his wife and her happiness. The last 20 or so years of their lives together were the most effervescent, connected and loving I have seen them. My mum would constantly talk about how lucky she was as woman to have stumbled onto a such a loving and capable man. She talked about the general fate of women of her generation in Viêtnam and that sometimes choice is not something many these women had.

Dad, we will continue to look after Mum the way you did, but I'm not sure if we can prepare the phó for her to your standard. Dad was a maverick, always thinking and acting outside the box.

Like most Asian fathers, complete compliance was the order of the day, however my father particularly enjoyed probing at my young developing mind with philosophical debates about general matters and current events. This helped me forge independent reasoning and validating my own thoughts. I remember trying so hard to outwit this man with my clever arguments, not quite achieving it but wanting to do better next time.

Dad had this habit of constantly repeating his messages. It's like the Chinese water torture – sooner or later you'll break! One of the key messages he had for us growing up was the abundant opportunities and how lucky we are to have resettled in Australia. He would talk about us seizing our good fortune and contributing back to a community that had welcomed us with open arms when we were destitute.

He would also talk about the values of personal sacrifice and how to elevate the next generation so that they can stand on our shoulders. I tried to live my life according to those values' dad, sometimes I hit, sometimes I miss (forgive me for the times I missed).

He enjoyed intellectual conversations so much that even while during his last days on Earth, while I accompanied him to the radiography dept, the attending nurses and I had a robust discussion about past Australian prime ministers.

A Packet of Cigarettes

When we pushed him back to his ward, his last words to me were, "Not many people liked John Howard!"

He retained his cognition right to the end.

To sum up his life, from a place of destitution, he was self-reliant, ever evolving, his ingenuity helped him succeed at most of his vocations, from hairdressing, photographer, carpenter to businessman. His courage and skill-mastery allowed him to captain his family across the seas in search of freedom. His generosity and kindness are exemplified by his family members, close friends and rural Viêtnamese communities whose lives he had touched by his desire to help those less fortunate.

Dad, I'm forever grateful to have you as a father, I will honour your wish for us to all take care of each other and leave no one behind. I will support and love Mum and continue to try and teach my children the values that were impressed onto me.

You lived such a meaningful life. Those lessons and values that you have imparted will remain with me forever. We have it all covered here; you can move go to the next stage of your journey now. I have you in my heart always.

Con xe nho nhung loi dai ba da dai con. Con xe noi guong cua ba de lam nguoi. Con gang lam nguoi mau tot nhut cho chau ngoai cu ba, de con dieu giac dang tre. Con mai mai thuong ba.

Translation: I will remember the lessons you have taught us. I will model you as a picture of responsibility to guide the next generations. I will love and cherish you forever.

Chris

My father's presence in our lives has left an indelible mark of kindness, humility, and progressive values. My father was a man rooted in tradition, yet forward-thinking in his beliefs.

The Children's Eulogies to Thiêu

Coming from a patriarchal society, he championed gender equality, ensuring that his son and daughters were given the same opportunities – clearly as you can all see, Dad was right. You just have to look at Jennifer, Dianne and Joanne to see that anything can be achieved.

He believed in the inherent worth of every individual, regardless of gender, and this progressive stance shaped our family into what it is today. In a world often divided by social issues and lifestyle choices, my father was a beacon of understanding and acceptance. He might not have always grasped the beat of those who danced differently, but he would listen intently, striving to join in once he could follow.

His ever-evolving perspective taught us the value of acceptance, patience and the importance of supporting your family. When you were family to my dad, he never gave up on you. I can attest to that personally. His unwavering commitment to us was a source of strength and comfort, a constant reminder that we were never alone in our journeys. A humble man, my father always put the needs of others before his own.

About 12 years ago, my sisters and I decided to gift our parents first-class plane tickets for a trip around the world. We were eager to hear about the luxury and comfort they experienced. Upon their return, their response was simple yet profound: 'It was a great experience but once was enough.' They asked us to save money on future flights and invest it in their philanthropic projects instead.

One such project was the building of a crematorium in Bac Lieu, the village where they met – a testament to their love and dedication to giving back to the community.

Today, as we celebrate his life, let us remember my father as a man who embraced change, fostered equality, and dedicated himself to the well-being of others. His legacy lives on in the values he instilled in us, the love he shared, and the positive impact he made on everyone that he met in the 82 years.

Thank you for everything you've done for us Dad, your work here is done. Please give Grandma Trúóng a hug from all of us.

Joanne

Dad lived simply. With no formal education, he shared with us simple lessons for a good life.
- Respect others, respect yourself, and others will respect you.
- Family is important – always take care of your family.
- Learn to recognise the good in people and help those who need it.
- Don't be wasteful with food or resources – think of their true cost.
- Treat people well when they are alive and you won't need to mourn them when they pass on.

He managed to achieve so much. Orphaned at a young age with little hope for a good future, he led this family through times of danger, uncertainty, and poverty, reinforcing each step of the ladder to support the climb.

Dad always had time for his grandkids – he and Mum would delight in watching the kids enjoy their home-cooking, hearing about their lives, hobbies and interests. Anything he found a little unusual or amusing he'd grin, click his tongue and shake his head.

Dad was a great teacher to those around him, but always a student himself. He reinforced these values but also lived them. His capacity and willingness to learn new skills in dancing, music, technology, gardening and cooking meant that he was always discovering, experimenting and bringing joy to those around him.

The Children's Eulogies to Thiêu

The amazing love story between him and Mum was something I only appreciated as an adult. That good relationships were not a given and that sacrifices were needed for benefits to be reaped. Theirs was the best I have ever seen, one of selflessness, patience, good humour and a pinch of spiciness.

One of the early stories shared about my childhood was when I was a baby and when my dad came back from long periods of work away from home, all he wanted to do was hold me, and apparently, I cried a lot when he did. He became so frustrated he would smack me. Gave me something to cry about.

He told to me this story often. Every time I heard it, I wished I could go back in time and enjoy those hugs he so wanted back then. But never as much as I do now.

The Garden You Leave Behind

Thank you for the Garden you leave behind,
Ever growing, ever improving,
Soil once forgotten flourished and bloomed,
A legacy that will continue to live on.

The fruits shared with many and more,
Giving nourishment, giving strength,
A family trellis to provide support,
Keeping your precious safe from harm.

You grew possibilities and aspirations,
Fertilised with kindness and caring,
Intelligent bravery and platinum resolve,
We cherish your Garden, your wisdom entwined.

We will miss you, Dad.

About the Author

MIKE WHEELER IS A JOURNALIST/EDITOR and has written for sport, travel, consumer technology and business-to-business publications and online portals.

Notes

www.ingramcontent.com/pod-product-compliance
Lightning Source LLC
Chambersburg PA
CBHW042045280426
43661CB00094B/1038